Notes on Training

Dear Jennifer

Notes on Training

Tsutomu Ohshima

Tsutomu Ohshima

Pine Winds Press

PO Box 720, Ravensdale, WA 98051

Pine Winds Editor: Thomas M. Blaschko

ISBN 0-937663-32-8

Contents

Forward

This book is a collection of practice notes published in the Shotokan Karate of America newsletter from 1965 to 1995. I want to thank all of the people who transcribed the notes for the newsletters over the years, including Jim Sagawa, Albert Kubota, Chris Hunt, Tom Muzila, Michael Sellmer, Jon Fledderjohann, Andrew Foote, Cathy Cleveland, Natalie Severdia-Abboud and Bridgette Culligan.

It is my sincere hope that this collection of notes will help students now and in the future practice seriously in the traditional martial art of karate. It is just a simple book to explain some of the points I think are important when you are making kata or basics or sparring. If it helps you with your practice, then I am glad.

Tsutomu Ohshima
Santa Barbara, California
April 26, 1998

Introduction

Before I talk about the parts of practice, it is important to look at what we are doing in training, to think about the real reason why we practice. In Japanese the word is keiko. The character "kei" means to think and "ko" means old or ancient. So practice, keiko, means to think of the ancient, that is to think back to the masters.

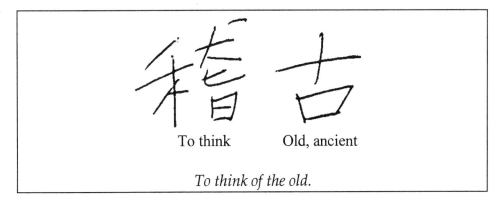

To think   Old, ancient

To think of the old.

When we practice, this is what we do. We try to understand the lessons the masters of the past have transmitted to us through the katas (forms) and more recently through the basics and methods of sparring described by

Master Funakoshi. This book has some of my ideas about what these masters were trying to show us with their practice. I have tried to make clear explanations but some things are beyond words. The only way to figure them out is to practice seriously for many years. If you practice well, you will find them for yourself.

When you are trying to solve a problem in practice, sometimes much practice is required. You must be conscious of the problem day and night, and try to find the best way. Stick with it until you overcome it. In this way you will be making a discovery just like the ancient masters did and this is a great feeling.

One of the greatest parts of martial arts is that at the same time we are polishing our physical movements, we are also polishing our minds and thus becoming better persons. We can become strong and good at the same time. In original martial arts the idea was simple — to win a battle — and everyone sought to become very harsh, cruel, almost inhuman, to achieve this aim. But at the highest level, the person with the cleanest mind won, and that is the really beautiful part of martial arts.

We are not practicing just to learn techniques. We are also searching for our strongest feeling and ideal mentality. No matter what we are doing, the most important element is our mental strength. So that is what we do in our daily practices and special trainings: find our best mentality, how we can face difficulties any time, any place, against any opponent.

There is an old explanation of Zen which also serves to explain martial arts practice. The simple Japanese characters on the next page illustrate the meaning of our practice.

The beautiful part of our mind is easily lost and easily collects dust; therefore, it must be constantly polished. We must bring this part of the mind up to the ideal human level. This is manifesting the Buddha in yourself in this lifetime.

As karate practitioners, we are looking for this serious mental and physical training for ourselves, but we know that is not enough. Simultaneously we have to be realistic and effective in combat. We have to be able to face not only amateur attacks, but also the attacks of other strong karate practitioners.

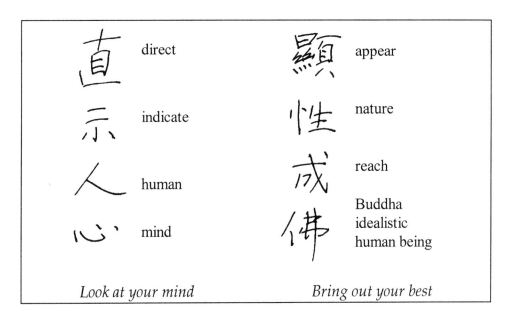

直 direct	顯 appear
示 indicate	性 nature
人 human	戒 reach
心 mind	佛 Buddha idealistic human being

Look at your mind   *Bring out your best*

Look at your own mind severely, directly and honestly. That is the first way to find the human mind. Look at your own, from bottom to top. This is our training process. The mind is sometimes good, sometimes bad, ugly or beautiful, cowardly or courageous.

Once we look at our minds, the real deep parts of the mind come out. The beautiful, clean, powerful part of the mind comes out after the bad part is examined and removed.

For example, you cannot escape the punch of a strong opponent by thinking you should escape it or by thinking you need to perform some twist of your stomach to get out. You must learn, instead, to extend your mentality into your opponent as he attacks. You can't have an empty stomach feeling, sucking in to avoid the attack. Your stomach should be full, connected with your breathing. Then even if the attack brushes your stomach, it will not hurt you.

You will learn this only through practice. You must face many opponents and many attacks. You must make 10,000 or more of your favorite kata before you begin to understand its true meaning. You must practice your favorite technique 100,000 times before you can use it in any situation, against any opponent. Think of this: if your opponent has made 100,000 oizuki thinking of a realistic situation every time, do you think you can escape if you haven't practiced at least that many times?

Our practice stands on realistic combat. We have to know we are standing on the Earth with two legs and, when an opponent comes to jump on us, no matter what, we've got to destroy him. What do I mean, "Destroy the opponent?" I mean destroy the opponent's evil mind. You must be able to use every part of your body and mind to stop his evil mind.

The words in this book are to guide you, but the practice is something you must make for yourself, honestly and straight, if you want to understand what karate really is.

Kata (Forms)

Katas, also called forms, are sets of twenty to sixty or so continuous techniques which represent combat against a set of opponents. These katas were created by the masters and geniuses in the past to transmit their ideas and understanding to later generations. Katas hold crystals of knowledge which are passed down from senior to junior. Even if someone makes some mistakes in transmitting a kata, it still retains some feeling from the person who created it.

In the beginning of Shotokan, everybody asked Master Funakoshi how many katas do you know, what is next and so on. I experienced the same thing when I started to teach outside of Japan. Many people came who wanted just to memorize the order of the forms. They would ask me how many katas I knew and tell me that they knew some guy that knew 100 katas. The same thing happened when Master Funakoshi went to Tokyo and he had to say that he knew 60 or 80 or however many he knew.

Maybe he knew the order of this many forms, but he also knew that the purpose of kata practice is not to memorize the order of the forms or to make a collection of the many orders and variations. And also, he knew that all the experts, the Masters in Okinawa before his period, knew only a few katas each. They trained in their few, favorite katas their whole life. Therefore, most of them knew only one or two.

Maybe Master Funakoshi was one of the exceptions. He knew maybe ten, maybe less. But before he left the Okinawan Islands, he visited his friends and many experts and collected many katas just to introduce them to the people in Tokyo when he went there in 1922.

When he established Shotokan after a certain number of years, he had to be honest with his pupils and he started to say that to memorize the order of the katas is not the real kata practice. That is why, if you open Master Funakoshi's **Karate-Do Kyohan**, he emphasizes that it's kind of a criticism of himself that he brought lots of different katas into Tokyo. Some of my seniors, they are so happy to collect many different katas, and they think that's kata practice. I've seen this many times.

The problem is if you know 40 or 50 katas, and even if you make each one only 2,000 times, you've still got to do 100,000 katas. One kata 2,000 times is not enough to master anything. It was a fashion to memorize lots of katas but Master Funakoshi thought that was not the direction for karate practice.

Therefore, I'm keeping his word in **Karate-Do Kyohan**, because I had the same experience when I left Japan. Master Funakoshi said that even our 18 katas may be too much. If you memorize the order of the forms and you do one or two as your favorite kata, that's the way to practice. If you practice one kata five to ten thousand times, you will start to realize this. Actually I took quite a long time to understand the Tekki forms. I cannot say five or ten thousand times is enough but less than that is not enough.

Katas were originally the only method of practicing in karate. Later we divided katas into basic techniques, to improve each stance, each movement of our hips, each block and attack, or to learn how to kick with a strong standing leg and so forth. Later we wanted to apply katas with partners to prepare for real combat, so we invented kumite. But all our basics, all our kumite, everything comes from the katas.

With a kata we can practice together with our friends and we can push ourselves beyond our own limits. We can also practice katas for many years, even though, sometimes, we don't want to practice anything. If you memorize the order of a form and get used to it, if you like it, you can continuously face yourself and polish yourself through kata practice. After a certain age, I'm sure most senior black belts realize that without kata practice, we cannot continue to practice.

In my viewpoint, since katas exist in karate as a martial art, we should not make up some flashy or fashionable exaggerations of the movements that are not realistic. In the 1940s and 1950s in the university dojos in Japan, most instructors were in their early 20s. Although they were quite capable in kumite, the maturity in kata was not there. Therefore, there was some misunderstanding and theatrical mentality and they exaggerated certain movements in the katas. These days there are kata competitions where the judging is not quite at a good level and where movements are often made slower or quicker to impress the judges or the audience. For instance, the first movements in Heian Yodan became slower and slower. When I learned the kata, these movements were only a little bit slower than Heian Nidan.

We must remember clearly that each movement has to be realistic. We cannot make changes or exaggerate movements in the katas to impress the general public. Instructors have to make sure each movement in the kata conforms to Master Funakoshi's textbook and is executed exactly as Master says. But you'd be surprised, there are many incomplete parts in these katas. Still, we practice them as Master Funakoshi wrote in his book, both the good parts and the incomplete parts, many thousands of times until we really understand them. Knowing what is not right in a form is a good lesson, too. These notes use **Karate-Do Kyohan** as a reference. The movement numbers here correspond to the movement numbers in the Master's book.

Kata is realistic combat formalized into exact lines so that we can repeat the same motions over and over. We should have strict and strong eyes to look at ourselves. What kind of stance are we making? What kind of back foot are we making? If an opponent sweeps our front leg, how do we continue to fight? And when we block, is it realistic against the opponent's particular attacking techniques? When we execute a technique, is it the strongest, best kime (focused energy) we can make or not? Even as we do the kata over and over, always in the deep parts of our mind we are seeing realistic situations and realistic combat.

For instance, no matter how many times I tell someone not to do it, they still attack with open legs, open stomach, open neck, open nose and expose many vital points. So we make this kind of educational program where we always have to be conscious of not exposing our centerline and staying on the line.

The most important point to be emphasized is how to develop a straight, strong mind with the eyes. Look directly at your opponent, not down or away. This will help make the mind straight, strong and alert. This is why we emphasize the eyes as being of primary importance.

When we find difficult or complicated parts of a kata, we have to repeat them many times. Some parts of the kata are very easy. Some parts are very difficult. If some parts of the kata make you feel uncomfortable, pick these as a special practice and repeat them much more than the easier parts. We are always looking at ourselves to make ourselves better. This is the important point in kata practice.

The start of the kata is the most important moment. When you stand in shizentai or some other yoi form, your mind has to be in all directions. In other words, you don't have any particular idea or direction, but your mind is alert. Then, the moment when you start, your strong feeling goes to the first opponent and your eyes and hips start to move in that direction. The first technique comes naturally from this initial movement.

And remember we are always training for a real situation, and I hope all senior members can make katas not just in the dojo, but anywhere, some place rocky or muddy or on a beach. Of course, we don't teach beginners in a rocky place. That practice is the seniors' personal project.

When we repeat a kata, it's not just to memorize the order of the form. We have to digest each movement, and this takes at least several thousand times. First we memorize the order of the form. If you pass 1,000 times, your kata is getting much better than before. If you pass 2,000 times, your kata is becoming more powerful as you learn what we're doing with each technique. If you've got 3,000 times, your kata looks much better with effective and realistic blocks and kicks and punches. Then we start to learn not only realistic blocks and attacks, but the rhythm and tempo, the slow and quick and the hard and the soft and where we contract and expand our body. After 5,000 times, your kata starts to become your own kata.

Still that is not everything, so we learn how to make ideal breathing without the explanation of instructors, each of us finding out for ourselves how to make breathing correctly. We learn to make kiai — each kata usually has two — with the strongest breathing in the kata. And then after a few years, we start to feel what the masters or experts felt who invented the kata. We start to feel what these geniuses, who practiced the kata for many years, were trying to transmit to us.

And though we follow what they are saying to us through kata practice, still we find our own feeling, our own rhythm, our own interpretations. Then finally, we reach the level where we can express our strongest, finest energy in the kata. Even though each one of us makes the same kata, without any change or any particular movements, we still have our own unique kata. I think that is our kata practice.

Taikyoku Kata (First Cause)

Taikyoku means first cause or the original force in the universe before there was any form. A few of my senior members think that the Taikyoku katas are very important to practice although I don't lead them very much. Master Egami, one of my most respected seniors, felt that the Taikyoku katas were the ideal form and should be practiced the most. One of his favorite practices was to execute Taikyoku Shodan within fifteen seconds, which is like running all the way.

As with many things in karate, you must decide for yourself if these very simple forms are the right ones for you to practice. However, if you feel this way, I suggest that you learn at least one of the advanced forms very well. Do it more than 10,000 times before you come back to the Taikyoku katas.

Heian Kata (Peaceful Mind)

Heian means peaceful mind. Master Funakoshi felt that after mastering these forms, practitioners could be confident about defending themselves in most situations. The name, peaceful mind, comes from this feeling of confidence.

The Heian katas came from Master Anko Itosu during the time he was teaching karate in the Okinawa schools. In the early 1900's he decided that the katas he knew were too difficult for his students to learn so he developed the five simpler katas which he called Pinan.

The last four Heian katas were a new kind of training when Master Itosu reorganized them but I think Heian Shodan is actually much older. I once saw a southern Chinese practitioner demonstrate a kata almost identical to Heian Shodan so I am sure that katas like Heian Shodan have existed for many years. Everyone practicing katas like these shares the same roots. Other styles, including Wado-kai, Tang Soo Do and Taekwondo, do them in exactly the same order. These katas are a direct line to Master Funakoshi or to Master Itosu before him.

When Master Funakoshi went to Japan, he changed the name from Pinan to Heian and switched the order of the first two katas. I don't know why Heian Shodan was Pinan Nidan since Heian Shodan is obviously a much simpler form. To me it seems very natural to use Master Funakoshi's order.

When we study the Heian katas, one important aspect to consider is the rhythm and speed. When we first begin to practice, we are very clumsy and slow and have great difficulty balancing and making a strong stance. Later, after some practice, we are more stable and we're happy to move more quickly. At this point some people can finish Heian Shodan within 16 seconds.

But after we begin to practice seriously, always imagining a real situation and gaining experience with kumite, we realize that speed is not objective, but subjective. In other words, speed is the result of a particular atmosphere between you and your opponent. People's mentalities, emotions, physical size, weight, past experiences and personalities are all elements that play a part in the perception of speed in physical movements.

Each opponent and observer of a kumite match will have a very different impression about the speed of the movements. Your actual speed is of secondary importance to your opponent's impression of your movements and speed. Ancient martial artists observed that speed does not exist by itself. Quick movements appear fast in relation to slow movements. This understanding of relative speed is illustrated especially in Heian Godan when we make some parts quickly and other parts slowly.

When someone is just starting, they can start with any of the Heian katas because the techniques are all the same level. The first kata doesn't have to be Heian Shodan.

Heian Shodan

Heian Shodan was originally an orthodox practice and should be kept exactly as it was meant to be. This is the original Shaolin form, our favorite kata practice. It is a very authentic kata and every move must be done and expressed with a big, dynamic, clean feeling.

Heian Shodan is one of the oldest katas, maybe 800 to 1,000 years old. Schools in South China and in Okinawa have katas that are very similar to Heian Shodan. Master Anko Itosu, Master Funakoshi's direct teacher, reorganized all the Heian Katas about 100 years ago to teach katas in schools in Okinawa. But Heian Shodan is the oldest Heian Kata, having originated somewhere in Southeast Asia.

For a thousand years, many masters practiced this one kata, the simplest one, and every time they found something different. Throughout their whole life they tried to polish it. Therefore, instructors have to sincerely, seriously try their best when showing this kata and practicing with junior members.

When we study Heian Shodan, I hope everybody experiences a new, fresh viewpoint, not "Oh, we're doing the same thing over again." We have to always try to look at katas, and ourselves, from different viewpoints. Otherwise we miss some understanding of the kata. And if we miss some opportunity to look at ourselves, we're missing the purpose of our life.

We think, "Oh, I know this kata." But we *don't* know it. Every time we make this form, in every kata, we have to find some new element. We must never let ourselves feel comfortable. This kata, because it is so basic, is one of the most difficult katas, I think. So each movement has to be ideal, realistic and clean. Each kata has to be unified, with one feeling.

We have to remember: nobody can make a perfect Heian Shodan yet. Still, that is our goal, to make the perfect, complete Heian Shodan. One block, one stance, each has to be polished, refined, made perfect and realistic and then beautiful. That's Heian Shodan practice.

When you do the kata, emphasize the first movement. Since about 1989, we have practiced basics to the side, making gedan barai or maete. This is the same movement as the first movement in Heian Shodan. Someone who has practiced Heian Shodan for many years starts to realize that this first movement is the ideal movement to many directions, not just to the side. You should be able to make this movement to the front and at all angles.

I would like to explain the most important parts of this first movement. When you stand in shizentai (natural stance), your starting form, your mind has to be aware of things in all directions. In other words, you don't have any particular idea or direction, but your mind is alert. Then, the moment when you start, your strong feeling goes to the opponent on your left and your hips start to move naturally. The movement of your hips is not turning, but opening to the left. The mind goes first and then your eyes follow with your hips, then stepping and blocking hand and pulling hand, all together. To make this movement freely, your back foot has to turn to the left as you step. In other words, the back leg has to connect with the down block completely. If the heel or the side of the back foot goes up, this is not the right stance.

When we practice gedan barai or oizuki or maete to the side, I think we get a much clearer understanding of how to execute blocks or attacks at the moment the opponent decides to come destroy us. This is one of the most important elements, imagining your opponents and when they decide to attack, so that you don't have any hesitation, any minor motion, any unnecessary time between the moment they decide to start and your execution of the block or attack.

I think there is no difference between beginners and experts if your mind is alert. When your mind wakes up, everybody can do this move. One of the more difficult parts, one of the differences between senior and junior members, is understanding how hips follow your feeling. To move without any delay, without any minor motion, with the strongest feeling and most dynamic physical power, hips are the key. I hope everybody enjoys the first movements of Heian Shodan.

In the rest of the kata, keep low hips all the way. Every block, every oizuki, every ageuke, keep low hips, almost knee level. Stand with a strong back leg with the back toes in, and hold your balance and weight mainly with the back leg. Second, always keep your eyes level so you can not only see opponents in front of you but also stay aware of opponents to the side and behind. Your mind must be awake and while you are making this form, you are always conscious of your opponents. Before you turn, always feel somebody coming from behind. Third, keep your pulling hand always on the hip bone and your underarms slightly tight. After you repeat Heian Shodan this way many times, your hips will start to move.

I hope everybody can make a low zenkutsu stance, and not forgive yourself when you make a higher, more comfortable stance. If you feel that you can do a very good Heian Shodan, try it again with your stance a half inch lower. Then you will find out how much you can do. Keep going down until your hips are knee high throughout the whole kata.

To learn this low stance, step to the side many times with gedan barai, just like Heian Shodan's first movement to the left. This first movement sets the level of the hips for the rest of the kata (except one time, in the fourth movement of Heian Shodan, when the hips go up). All other hips have to be at the same level as the first movement. Remember that you stand with the back leg mainly.

Make the proper stances and attack with one feeling. The three attacks in movements 14-16 should be done with more of a pause between the first and second than between the second and third.

One day perhaps you can apply the techniques from Heian Shodan to a real situation. Somebody starts to attack and your gedan barai destroys the opponent's leg or arm. Then you make your best oizuki and finish the fight. Even in this simple kata remember to look for realistic applications.

Heian Nidan

Heian Nidan was a very popular kata in the Okinawan Islands at the time Master Itosu reorganized the Heian katas and many people practiced it. Emphasis was on the remarkable switching and shifting hips to change the stance from kokutsu (back stance) to zenkutsu (front stance) and back to kokutsu. When I was young, I liked Heian Nidan and I practiced a lot of this form. I think when we are young, we should make lots of Heian Nidan.

When I began to practice Heian Nidan, we started with fudodachi (immovable) stance from the beginning. At that time Master Funakoshi's son, Yoshitaka Funakoshi, I think he was the fourth son of Master Funakoshi, liked to practice fudodachi and he created the idea of practicing fudodachi in basics and even in katas. Of course, we now practice zenkutsu and kokutsu dachi as Master Funakoshi wrote down in **Karate-Do Kyohan**.

In this kata many people pay attention to the hand movements, but the stance is most important. You have to make your stance with strong hips, legs and, especially, feet. Otherwise the blocks and punches don't work. Don't let your movements shrink. Execute this kata with dynamic movements and a big feeling.

There are very interesting stances, many kokutsu stances and you have to emphasize making a solid stance each time. If you make a strong stance a habit early in your training, after many years your karate becomes very solid. But if you don't make the right stance in the beginning, you have to suffer for a long time. Therefore, in each movement be cautious about your stance, especially brown belts.

Among the Heians, I think Heian Nidan is a good kata and one of the most balanced. The only problem is the side up kick in movement eight. Doing that kick with the side edge of the foot has caused many Shotokan practitioners to hurt their lower backs. You have to make this side up kick carefully, as we are doing right now, kicking with the toes like a front kick to the side.

The first movements of Heian Yodan and Heian Nidan are very similar. In the first movement of Heian Nidan we block an opponent's upper level attack from the left. The body is facing to the front and the head is turned to the left. Many people keep their feet in the original position of the starting form, leaving the back toes pointing out, but you have to make back stance with the right leg, with your left leg free from your weight and balance. Shift your weight onto the back leg while simultaneously pushing your right toe in. Your right heel has to be very strong to stand in back stance against the opponent to your left. Also, the position of the arms should be exactly correct. Many people think they are doing these movements correctly, but they should practice in front of a mirror and see what they are really doing.

The third movement in Heian Nidan is actually maete (jab) from back stance. This is a very difficult technique. When you learn maete, I think it's better to stand with front stance. However, when we make the kata, we have to keep the traditional order and techniques exactly as we learned them.

When you turn to the right (movement 4), shift your weight to the left side to make kokutsu against an opponent from the right. As you complete the difficult shifting of weight from right to left, your left toe has to go in and your left heel has to be very strong to make kokutsu against the pushing power of the opponent to your right. At the same time you are free to kick with the front foot or lift it against an opponent's sweeping attack. It is a good idea to practice the stance, the right-leg kokutsu and then the shift to the left-leg kokutsu until you get the idea. This shifting is actually done with the hips, but hips and feet go together. If you can't see these little things, watch your seniors' practice carefully to catch them. Originally, these difficult points were secret movements in the katas. Masters and experts hid these kinds of things. That is because understanding of these movements is the key to footwork in kata practice. We always move and keep our balance with the back leg, back foot and back ankle.

There is one part many people are not doing correctly, the seventh movement after you make a half-step up with the left foot and before you execute the side up kick and backfist to the back. Here the wrist of your left hand (the pulling hand) goes down to your left hipbone, not in front of your body. Tighten your left underarm (especially the latissimus dorsi muscle) and put the right fist onto the left fist. Some people don't have the left fist on the hipbone or don't touch both fists. Then they execute the attack to the back in the eighth movement with opening arms. That is not right. The pulling hand should be in the normal pulling-hand position and the elbow must be in. Side up kick here can only be realistic and effective with a strong left standing leg, with the hip stabilized by the left underarm and shoulder. You need to concentrate on making a solid pulling hand that does not move when you kick and punch. Keep the shoulders down and the pulling underarm tight to make the technique work. This is actually not a realistic motion, but it is there to develop a strong stance and stabilize the hips and connect the opposite side underarm with the uraken. This kind of training is very useful for beginners to help them learn to execute uraken and kicks with a strong stance.

When beginners first learn these movements, you can tell how long they have practiced. Only people who have trained long enough and whose bodies have started to move can execute it very well. Somebody who has never practiced karate is very awkward. So this awkward and unrealistic movement has a very important purpose in training. I hope you practice this part until you feel comfortable executing the kick to the back.

Everywhere in the kata, before every turn, always be aware of the opponent behind you. At the end of the kata (movements 25 and 27) when you are making ageuke after gedan barai, always begin with an upper level, open hand block with the front arm. What you are doing is grabbing the opponent's arm and breaking the opponent's elbow with your ageuke. Therefore, the grabbing-pulling hand comes back to the hip *inside* the blocking hand. During this blocking motion, the wrists cross in front of your face, the pulling hand on the inside and the blocking hand on the outside. Many people are not clear on this part.

Heian Sandan

Heian Sandan is the shortest of the Heian series. Older members and people who do not have much stamina will find it much easier to do many repetitions with the young people. Since Heian Sandan can be done within 30 seconds and it is very interesting, I think we can repeat it many times.

Many women pick this kata as their favorite because of the dynamic hip movements in it. I think this is a good kata for women to study and practice for a while.

In Heian Sandan, we emphasize escaping techniques from opponents catching your wrist, catching your body from behind, catching your neck and so forth. These techniques are hard to visualize so it is important for you to practice escapes against a real opponent as you are learning this kata. Everybody has to execute exact techniques. If you don't make exact techniques, escaping techniques won't work.

One of the escapes I think is especially interesting is in the movements after the nukite. In that move (movement 9) we escape a grab of the attacking hand. The escape looks like the wrist goes to the hip, but in relation to the opponent, the hip actually goes to the wrist. In other words, if you are a small person against a larger opponent, don't try to pull your hand or arm away. Instead, when you turn, leave your wrist in place and move your hips to your wrist. Then when your wrist touches your hip, strike with the left tetsui to the opponent's elbow or to the side of the opponent's body. Don't escape with the power of the arm. Completely remove your conscious power from the wrist, shoulder and arms, but make your movements with a full breathing. Make your full feeling go into the arm and the wrist. Then use your hip movements and you can get out.

Another interesting thing we can learn from this kata is a distinctly different way of making gedan barai. Making gedan barai while facing the opponent in front of you and swinging the block down (as in movement 2) is different from swinging the block to the side as in movement 1 of Heian Shodan. When you face the opponent in front of you, you use the width of your body. The power of this block comes from rotating the hips to the front together with the swinging block. In contrast, when you swing the block down to the side, you are opening, not rotating, the hips. Instead of rotating, the form in Heian Shodan moves in one direction. So the hip, arm, in fact, the entire body and mind, move in one direction. Blocking to the side with a long stance and open hips is typical of the Shaolin influence. Blocking with a rotating hip as in Heian Sandan is a Shokei technique.

Heian Sandan seems to combine the influences of both the Shaolin and Shokei schools. My impression is that this kata, compared with the other Heians, has a stronger Shokei influence. Heian Sandan is not like Heian Nidan or Heian Shodan. In Heian Sandan, the opponent is much closer to you, so it is a good kata to train for close combat, where somebody is holding your arm or grabbing you and jumping on you. You should practice Heian Sandan with lower hips and with a solid stance.

You must make a good kokutsu in the first and fourth movements, keeping the back foot in, the body facing to the front, with only the head turned left or right.

Other stances are very important, especially the kibadachi and the standing heisoku dachi (close-legged stance) in movement 11. Put your feet together and stand. Then in movements 12 to 14 suddenly stamp, making kibadachi with a strong block and back fist attack. Your mind must lead your body and your hips must go forward before stamping, otherwise you can't make a solid kibadachi.

Heian Sandan has three stamping movements (12, 15 and 18). Unfortunately, we cannot stamp on the floor of the dojo every time we make basic fumikomi. If we could do it, in a way it would be more natural. But Heian Sandan's fumikomi is a little different from what we are doing when we make basic fumikomi. Sometimes it's better to touch the ground as long as we don't hurt our feet or legs or hips. If we always kick in the air, some people never realize that, when we kick and actually make contact, sometimes power comes back to our body and the kick doesn't work. On the other hand, if you stamp too strongly every time, sometimes it hurts your heels or ankles, so it is very difficult to determine how much you can and cannot stamp. You must be careful not to get injured either way — one, because of not kicking realistically; and two, because of stamping too strongly every time or too many times.

Heian Sandan emphasizes executing a hitting down uraken from kibadachi (movements 13, 16 and 19). The elbow on the uraken must pull down and connect with the kibadachi stance.

In movement 22, with the swinging right hand attacking the opponent's head behind you and the left fist pulling to the hip, this is not just a pulling hand, this is an elbow attack. You have to emphasize a strong elbow attack to the opponent behind you. This is followed (movement 23) by a dynamic sliding of the hips to the right with both feet, while at the same time attacking behind you with the right elbow. When attacking with the fist to the opponent's head behind you, the back of the fist is always up. Some people are not making this form correctly.

Throughout the kata, emphasize your mind leading your body as you move from kokutsu to zenkutsu, zenkutsu to kibadachi, heisoku dachi to kibadachi or when turning with the kibadachi. Each movement has to be realistic, dynamic and powerful. Make this kata strongly and never lose your balance.

Heian Yodan

The rhythm or speed of Heian Yodan is not exactly the same as it was fifty or one hundred years ago. Originally the first movement was not slow, but just like Heian Nidan. That's what Senior Watanabe told me. Up until the 1940s people were still executing the opening movements of this kata, open hand morote-uke, with both hands blocking quite quickly. Then students in Tokyo started getting slower and slower, some people quite slow.

I remember that when I started in the 1940s, the first movements were made very slowly, with almost a theatrical effect. The younger generation thought this was the correct way, but people who practiced with Master Funakoshi before the 1940s said that these first movements were the same speed as the first movements in Heian Nidan. Therefore, we have to try to make these movements at the original speed — but not very quick either, especially after the first movement when the hands go down, before making the second movement. The speed, of course, depends on our own mentality, our own interpretation, our own level of understanding. So we don't know exactly how quick or how slow, but we have to be careful that we are not making some artificial, extremely slow movement.

There are many open hand techniques in Heian Yodan. When we open our hands, it's very easy to break our fingers and thumb. Throughout this kata you have to be conscious of each fingertip. For example, in the first two movements of the kata and, later, when you are executing shuto (sword hand), your breathing always has to come to the finger tips. Don't separate your fingers.

Some people, from the yoi stance, move their hands to the right a bit and then block to the left. This is incorrect. Move the hands directly from the yoi position in front of the thighs to the left blocking position. After this, both hands come down then rise directly to block an attack from the right. Also, recent study indicates that there is some possibility that this kokutsu-dachi stance and block to the side in Heian Nidan is an attack with two arms, a blocking attack to the side. The open hand block in Heian Yodan may not look like an attack, but this could be a simultaneous block and attack with both hands.

When you execute uraken to the side (movement 6), the important point is the pulling side underarm. This pulling side underarm is never open and the pulling underarm never moves, the shoulder never goes up and the pulling hand stays on the hip. This is because side up kick and uraken connect with the opposite side of the hips. So in this part, the pulling underarm should be tight from the beginning so you can continue smoothly with the right elbow attack (movement 7). Here, the right shoulder should be down, right underarm should be tight and you should push the right hip in as much as you can. The next movements (9 and 10) in the opposite direction are the same.

After executing enpi (movement 10) to the right side, look and block to the front (movement 11). First, the right hand covers your face completely against an attack from the left side. Then switch to block with the left hand and make a big swinging motion with the right hand, coming to the front with the elbow extended and make shuto (sword hand attack) to the opponent's temple or neck. Don't bend the elbow, extend it. This right hand makes a big motion, but never goes behind the line of the shoulders, beginning 90 degrees from the point where you attack with shuto.

The ageuke with open hands and shuto strike are not like the swinging motion in Kwanku. This time the shoulders have to be square. Don't put the right shoulder in front. In this kime (method of focusing our power) both standing knees straighten and buttocks tighten. At this moment the open hand which is striking connects with your stance and your breathing comes to the edge of your hand. The underarm on the pulling side is tight, too. Because this is not a swinging motion with the hips like in Kwanku, the kime has to be clearly connected with the stance. I believe that the inventor of Heian Yodan wanted to transmit this kind of kime, one of the most effective kimes, where the tanden (the one point under the abdomen) connects with the whole body.

These points are not quite understood by young people, even in Japan, because they don't understand the efficiency or effectiveness of this kime. These movements, although they look stiff and not very impressive are ancient, secret points which are transmitted through the kata to the next generation. The difference between this kime and the kime in Kwanku has to be explained clearly as one of the most important understandings of kime.

After we execute the shuto, we execute maegeri (movement 12). Realistically, this maegeri has to be inside of the right hand because your opponent's head is to the left of your right shuto but in the kata we kick just beyond the right index finger. Right after the kick (in movement 13), don't forget that the open left hand extends, with the motion of grabbing the opponent and pulling him toward you. As you pull, make right hand uraken with the right hand coming back first inside of the left hand and then over your head and then down to the opponent's upper level. Finish in front of your mouth, simultaneously pulling your left hand to your hip as a hikite (pulling hand). Bend your knees, making nekoashi dachi, or cat leg stance, with the left knee touching the side of the right knee, so that you can stop.

Many people eliminate the left hand extension where we grab the opponent as we jump in and make uraken with the right hand. Many people are also opening up their face to the opponent when making uraken, swinging the arm to the side. You have to make a big movement with the right hand, swinging up and hiding your face with your elbow, before coming down with the uraken. These are quite realistic movements where you jump in, grab the opponent and make uraken to the face. We should not eliminate or make changes to these effective, strong movements.

After this movement, after turning to the back with kokutsu, the open hands make fists, fists stopping in front of both shoulders, both hands blocking to make kakiwake (movement 14). This is one of the escaping techniques everybody can apply in a real situation when the opponent starts to grab our collar. Open the two arms, keeping the elbows no wider than your body line, and connect the wrists with the hips. Remember to keep the elbows on the line of the body and execute this technique just at the moment the opponent starts to grab but before he is really holding on strongly.

After kakiwake, when you execute your right leg front kick (movements 15), while you are kicking, both hands stay where they are. Don't pull either hand back until the execution of the right maete, when the left hand goes back to the left hip.

Junior members, start to coordinate the legs and arms when you kick and punch with maegeri-maete (movements 15-17 and 19-21). You have to make maegeri-maete many times, and don't make it two separate motions, especially in your breathing. Right after you kick, don't stop and then punch. Before the kicking leg lands, right after you finish the front kick, you are already starting maete with a dynamic hip movement.

After the last morote-uke (double block), when you catch the opponent's head with your open hands (in movement 25), don't bend your fingers. Extend them straight then pull down, making a fist.

Many people are shifting into zenkutsu when grasping the opponent's head but in **Karate-Do Kyohan**, Master Funakoshi did not indicate a shift from back stance into front stance at the beginning of this movement. From back stance, just reach up to catch the opponent's head. Then the hips shift forward simultaneously with the knee attack to the opponent's face. These parts changed in the last half of the century partly because it's much easier for beginners to shift into zenkutsu before bringing the knee up. But this movement of the arms has to be executed without shifting your stance or leaning towards your opponent. There is no time to make zenkutsu. Then you shift into front stance, pulling the hands down, raising the knee higher than the fists. In that move you hold the opponent's head or hair and strike with your right knee. With a small person against a tall person, this technique is, of course, very unrealistic. Yet, if the opponent's stance is very low or they are leaning forward and their face comes down, you can attack with the knee. Or, if the opponent is standing higher, you can still jump up, like double kick, and maybe stand momentarily with one leg on the opponent's hip while you hold his head and attack with the opposite knee. These are two possibilities you can think about, to use the knee as a realistic kick.

When making Heian Yodan, emphasize the clear differences between the kokutsu and zenkutsu stances.

Heian Godan

Heian Godan is good for young people who can jump high and far and make a dynamic kata. But, be aware of the speed of the kata. Everybody wants to finish katas very quickly, especially beginners who are young and energetic. Somehow we feel we have accomplished something or understand the techniques when we do the katas quickly.

This is not the realistic perspective. Speed is not the objective in a fight. Speed exists between you and your opponent, in the mind. Quickness exists in slow movements; power exists in no power. There are slow and quick movements in this kata. Some parts you must execute slowly, and still keep your mind alert, like the third, sixth and fourteenth movements. If you take enough time mentally and physically to make these movements slowly with your breathing, then the quick parts of the kata come to life.

You never relax, even through the slow parts. Never show your breathing to other people. And though you are hiding your breathing through these slow movements, be sure to keep a strong, concentrated mind. With this feeling, you can study how to combine the human mental rhythm with the rhythm of physical movements.

There are many difficult parts to Heian Godan. The first is the kokutsu (back stance) in the opening move. When I was younger, we were not clear about the stance in the first two movements. We did both udeuke and gyakuzuki from fudodachi. But, as you can see in **Karate-Do Kyohan**, Master Funakoshi clearly says that both stances are kokutsu. Therefore, at the beginning of the kata, when you feel an opponent coming from the left, you have to make a very strong and definite kokutsu as you sink down and block and punch.

To make the stance, bend your rear knee and turn the toes of your right (rear) foot toward the opponent. The hips have to be in just a little from the vertical line of the rear heel. If your toes point away from your opponent you cannot make a strong stance. Don't shift the weight to the outside of the foot with the big toe up in the air, don't let the heel go up and don't let the hips go behind the rear heel. If you do any of these, the opponent's pressure can throw you off balance. Put the weight evenly on all parts of the foot, then make kokutsu. Tighten the muscles on the inside of the thigh to make a solid back stance. This is similar to the footwork and stance in the first movement of Heian Nidan, Sandan and Yodan. This movement is very difficult to make with the left forearm block. The left fist is shoulder high and not far from the body, connected to the underarm (especially the latissimus dorsi muscle).

The next attack is also difficult because it is from back stance. However this is a good practice to connect the punch with both underarms, with the hips and back leg. Keep your forearm horizontal to the ground, punching straight to the opponent's solar plexus. In the gyakuzuki, keep the pulling hand and forearm parallel to the floor. Some people bend the elbow of the punching arm, but actually it needs to be straight. Connect the back stance heel with the attacking hand through your strong underarm and hips. Emphasize the back leg, especially the back heel staying on the ground, and connect the leg with the execution of the gyakuzuki.

Many people shift into a fudodachi or zenkutsu when they make the gyakuzuki in the second and fifth movements of Heian Godan but both stances are actually kokutsu. We cannot change the stance. If you want to make an effective gyakuzuki, shift your hips just a little bit toward the direction of the punch, but the stance still has to be a strong kokutsu.

When you feel the opponent coming from the other direction (movement 3), you slow down a little bit. Slowly move the right (rear) foot to the left foot to make a feet together stance (heisoku). Bend your left elbow and hold the fist in the water flowing (mizu-nagare) position with the forearm slanting slightly downward. The fist extends a short way beyond the right side of the body to protect the solar plexus.

We call this the water flowing position because, if you placed a drop of water on the elbow, it would slowly run down toward the fist. The elbow never goes lower than the fist and the fist is never so low that the water could run down quickly. The wrist and fist are straight, not bent up or down, and follow the line of the arm. The forearm is one fist's distance from the chest and parallel to the line of movement. The body's line must be exactly parallel to the line of movement in this position, too.

When you execute the fourth movement, right arm udeuke with left leg kokutsu, turn the left toes in, bend the knee, tighten the muscles on the inside of your thigh and hold your whole body solid. When you make kokutsu, stand with the weight on the back leg with the hips just a little ahead of the rear heel. If you want to test your back stance, make sure that you can move your front leg to escape a sweep and resist a push from an opponent in the front.

As I said before, the speed of these movements is important, too. My impression is that the speed of this kata was much slower before, not because they executed the block or thrust very slowly, but because there were both slow and quick movements, and it was never too slow, never too quick. This relative speed, the difference between the slow and quick movements, is very important in Heian Godan. For example, the first and second movements are made quickly with one breath. The third movement, standing straight in the heisoku stance is quite slow and we don't move right away after we turn and face to the right. The fourth and fifth movements are made quickly, in one breath, with no time between the block and attack. Then the sixth movement, when you face the front before you start to move, is again quite slow as you mentally prepare for the next motion. These initial movements are very important in understanding Heian Godan.

The seventh through twelfth movements, ending with the oizuki, are one long, continuous sequence made with one feeling. We exaggerate these slow and quick movements to make the difference between them clear. Avoid making every move with the same rhythm, one, two, three, four, one, two, three, four. By learning the true rhythm of the kata we can learn from the masters and geniuses who in their lives had many experiences in combat.

Another point many people misunderstand is in the fourteenth movement when you move the arms as if drawing a bow, pulling the right fist to the hip and extending the left arm straight out to the side with the hand open. In the beginning of this movement, while standing in kibadachi, the right hand extends to the left in front of the body, while the left hand comes back *under* the right arm before extending out to the side. Many people are making this movement with the left hand coming back *above* the right arm. This is wrong. Also, many people during this movement are making a pulling hand with the right hand with the small finger going outward. You've got to tighten your small finger and twist your wrist inward.

After the right elbow attack (movement 16) when you block with both arms (movement 17), you are standing in nekoashi dachi, cat stance. Keep hips low with both knees tightly together or this form is very unstable and weak. Against a wrestler or judo-ka you can easily be thrown if you don't put your knees together tightly.

Another difficult part is the 18th movement, just before jumping, when you extend your right fist in an uppercut to the opponent's chin. When I was young, we kept a very low kokutsu before making the uppercut. For a short time in the 1940s and 1950s, people didn't straighten their knees. From nekoashi dachi, they would uppercut and then jump from bent knees.

Next people thought that they should straighten both knees with the uppercut and then just before the jump, bend the knees a little and jump right away. Of course, we can't add this extra movement. **Karate-Do Kyohan** says that at the end of the uppercut, we "support the entire weight on the *slightly bent* right leg."

I remember Master Funakoshi emphasizing that it's almost like standing up with both knees straight and the front leg, left toe, foot to fist, on a straight line. He showed squeezing the buttocks, then moving both legs up at the same time as the uppercut. I remember when Master Funakoshi was old, he didn't jump very high, but he extended both knees very clearly almost to the straight position.

We need to keep this ideal movement: legs bent with the block, extending using the power of the buttocks with the uppercut, leaving the right leg slightly bent so we can make the jump right away.

When jumping and landing at the second kiai (movement 19), it is possible for some older or overweight people to damage their knees. When you jump, don't open up your knees. Your knees are always touching and you should have strong pressure on both knees when you land. Your right calf muscle and left shin are the brake. The left shin presses strongly against the right calf to make you stop. And your left toes lightly touch the right heel from the outside. Hips never go lower than knee level, otherwise you will hurt your knees. When you land, hips and knees are horizontal, on the same level. When you block with nekoashi dachi at the end of the jump, the most important thing is that both knees have to be really tight together and you stand mainly with the right foot.

Young people should execute this jump with a big, dynamic feeling and be able to jump higher and farther. The move is performed as if you were jumping over a bo and is an excellent exercise for spring in the legs. Don't let any power rise up into your shoulders. Keeping your breathing down will help keep your shoulders and power down. The kiai is right before you jump.

The last motions in the kata (movements 21 and 23) are throwing techniques, not attacking the groin and grabbing. We, Shotokan members, misunderstood this for a long time. When I was young, nobody explained these motions as a throwing technique. Now we have to make it clear that these motions block a kicking attack and then throw the opponent. The hand goes to the front with the hand open above the front knee. Make sure this hand goes outside the line of the body, otherwise you cannot block the opponent's kick.

Heian Godan is a one-line kata, so you have to keep all movements on the line, especially the last throwing technique. Keep the rear arm, elbow, shoulders and front elbow all on the same line with the stance.

This is not a long kata, but we have to make it with clear, exact stances, from kokutsu to zenkutsu, then to kibadachi and nekoashi dachi, and then jump and nekoashi dachi again, and then front stance, back stance, then come up, and then back stance again. There is no stance in between, so be sure that each stance is clear with a strong standing leg.

Bassai (Penetrate a Fortress)

"Batsu" or "Patsu" means to penetrate, "sai" means a fort, like a little castle. To penetrate this strong fort means some sort of explosion of feeling.

Bassai is one of the key katas in Shotokan. All Heian katas come from Bassai and Kwanku so it is one of the origins of our katas. It is also the most powerful kata with its dynamic rotation of the hips. If you practice it many times, your body will start to move very dynamically.

I think everybody knows that Bassai comes from a bo kata. The long bo is from the floor to the end of your fingertips in length, if you extend your arm straight up. The jo, or short bo, extends from the floor to your armpit. Either way, there are very effective, realistic techniques we call jodo or bojutsu. They have very powerful thrusting techniques similar to oizuki, as well as swinging techniques which are just like swinging a baseball bat. The power of these swinging motions always comes from the rotation of the hips. The power never goes up to the shoulders, and the underarm always connects to the hips, and the hips connect to the strong stance.

Bassai maintains the bojutsu understanding of hip movements in the karate kata. Throughout Bassai we emphasize dynamic rotating hip movements. Although we are not carrying a bo, we execute all the rotating blocks and punches with powerful and dynamic rotation of the hips.

Bassai is a good kata to teach you how to use your hips and to train for real combat. It is also a very useful kata for persons with powerful bodies, but even a very light, small person using dynamic rotation of the hips, can face a bigger opponent. So, from beginning to end, you have to be conscious of your hips.

When you are young you should do as many Bassai as you can. If you have the opportunity to come watch Sunday brown belt practice, you know that they are making 25 to 50 Bassai every Sunday. I'm expecting everybody to finish 5,000 Bassai before taking the shodan examination. I have found [in 1992] that only ten or twenty percent of candidates reached 5,000 times before they go to the dan test, and I hope more candidates reach that level in the future.

Everybody should train in Bassai right after learning the Heian forms. Not only brown belts, but also white belts who have trained for about one year should try to memorize the order of the movements and get used to these longer forms. For beginners, Bassai may seem a little more complicated or longer, and you may suffer a little bit learning it, but then when you go back to the Heian katas, they will seem very short and much simpler so you can execute them very nicely. Sometimes try to challenge yourself by learning a difficult kata, then go back to the simpler katas. That makes your practice feel easier. If you are a white belt practicing this kata, you should start to count how many times you make it before you become a brown belt, and when you become a brown belt, keep counting until you make at least 5,000. That's the way I learned.

When we are practicing Bassai, we emphasize the movement of the hips, strong standing legs and smooth and dynamic movements. Be sure that all of the swinging and thrusting techniques in the kata connect to the hip movement. The mind goes first, then the hips and techniques follow. If the mind is not there, you can hurt your body. Black belts, especially, have to concentrate on using this kata to polish their strong hips.

Remember each time you practice that the start of the kata is very important. Originally, the starting form of the two hands meant sun and moon. The right hand is the sun and the left is the crescent moon. From a more realistic viewpoint, this is also showing that a one-hand block and attack is much weaker than a two-hand block and attack. So both hands go together, this is the indication.

When you make the opening move, you have to send out your strongest feeling. The feeling of the block is to break through a wall of opponents. To make this move you must bring the arms back, so at the same time raise your knee to protect your body. The knee moves straight forward so that when you land, the right knee and foot point straight to the front. At the moment of contact, focus the power of the dynamic hips movement in the blocking arm. The left hand stays in contact with the right arm during the whole technique and at the moment of contact the middle finger of the left hand is touching the bone just below the wrist.

The punches and forearm blocks in the first part of the kata (movements 8 to 13) are in natural stance. At one time we thought this was kibadachi, but actually the stance is higher. When Master Funakoshi first learned this kata, these movements were done as an attack followed by a rising block, ducking down to get out of the way of a punch. Master Funakoshi did not like this feeling of hiding or shrinking from the opponent so he changed the block and the stance so that we show a bigger feeling against the opponent. Now we make the kata using udeuke with the hips' power going into the opponent and the hips turned to protect the lower parts of the body. In this block you must combine two important elements. First, the block is from the inside to the outside so you can make this block and remain very close to the opponent. Second, the hips turn into the opponent and cut his weak line so that the following techniques are your strong line against your opponent's weak line. Also, from this position it is very easy to make counterattacks such as enpi or fumikomi.

The upper level double block (movement 22) must be done with both arms blocking together. The arms go up at medium speed together with the breathing. At the end you focus strongly at the point of the block with both knuckles just touching the forehead.

A few moves later (movement 27) you have just made a down block in kibadachi. Next the head turns to the left and the left arm swings out. When you make this move, be sure that the left arm crosses under the right as if your were removing an opponent's hand grabbing your sleeve. It is easy for an opponent to control you when he holds your clothing, so you must practice this move to begin to understand how to escape from this kind of grab.

The scooping blocks near the end of Bassai (movements 38 and 39) should be done from a low stance. Each time one knee should be bent and the other leg straight. The hips should be low, at about knee's height.

Finally, all movements must go together with your courageous mind, from top to bottom, with your feeling going to the lower abdomen (the tanden). Execute all movements with no conscious power in the shoulders. Elbows never stick out with the exception of the morote-uke, the upper block with both hands in movement 22. When executing morote-uke, the elbows go out to open the attacker's hands, but after that the elbows go in again.

Kwanku (Look at the Sky)

"Kwan" means to look up or see through. "Ku" means sky, emptiness, nothingness. So you can say simply, "look at the sky" (because when you start the kata, your hands go up) or in a more philosophical way, "seeing through emptiness" (with the feeling of seeing truth through emptiness, or something like that). This emptiness is not the absence of all thought, but the absence of egotistical thought, personal concerns, worrying about what is going to happen. When these useless thoughts are gone, the clean, strong awareness of what is really happening is in your mind instead. This is the meaning of Kwanku.

Originally, Kwanku was pronounced the way it is now spelled, but modern Japanese language has gotten lighter and lighter, until the "w" is silent and the kata is pronounced "Kanku."

Before Master Funakoshi renamed it, this form was called Kushanku. This was the name of the diplomatic person or attaché who came with the Chinese ambassador to the Okinawan Islands 150 years ago. That's what Master told us in 1950. Since then we have found out two things: that it was over 300 years ago (around 1660), and that this is not the name of the person. Kushanku cannot be the name. It would be very unusual as a Chinese name. So it is kind of a nickname or title that people used to name the kata. Kushanku is both the Chinese and Okinawan pronunciation, more or less, but mainland Japanese people pronounce it Koshokun. It's the same characters, but a different pronunciation.

Anyway, an attaché did come from mainland China to Okinawa and demonstrated this form. We imagine that the person who made this kata had to be very tall, with a slender build, who has very good jumping kicks, an extrovert, someone who could face eight opponents. Eight opponents means you can fight against many people, so it must have been a very strong person who made it. He practiced this kata his whole life and his pupils did it all their lives, too.

Many karate people learned this form from him and renamed it, but even in the Okinawan Islands there are many different ways to perform it. Some people divide it into two or three. For instance, there is Kushanku-Dai (big one), Kushanku-Sho (small one) and Kushanku Tomari (for a little town on the islands).

As you know, this was Master Funakoshi's last favorite kata. He was making Kwanku demonstrations after he became 70 years old. We saw his Kwanku many times. Of course, when I saw him, he could not make a double jump kick very high, but he was still doing Kwanku. So all Shotokan members should practice many Kwanku. I hope many people enjoy practicing this kata.

Kwanku is a very basic kata. Even though it is long, I still consider it a basic kata. Each movement has to be precise and, even though this is a long form, we should have rhythm and be able to make a unified kata. After making this kata many times, your body starts to follow your mind.

All shodans have to practice Kwanku 5,000 times before taking the nidan test, but even senior black belts have to polish Kwanku. (If you already did it 5,000 times, now challenge yourself to make 10,000.) Kwanku is a long kata and makes you very tired, but when you are young you should make many Kwanku. I don't recommend that those over 40 years old make too many Kwanku, but up to 20 times in one practice is okay. Everybody should be in good shape and older members have to learn to make Kwanku without tensing or using conscious power in the muscles, especially shoulder and arm muscles, which should be relaxed, and each technique should be executed full of feeling.

I don't think we have much trouble with the order of this kata, but if you find that some parts are more difficult, take these parts and repeat them many times before or after kata practice. With a group this is much easier. For example, I remember several movements from Kwanku, when you turn and go down and turn to make shuto-uke (movements 42-45), that we had to practice 50 to 100 times after two hours of practice. We did that part many times and later on everybody could do it without much trouble. So, if you have trouble with any parts, just repeat them many times. Don't miss any minor movements, and always try to make the exact form of the kata each time. This is the way to improve your kata.

There are typical Kwanku movements, for instance, after execution of the shuto attack and kick, after we get in and turn back. In this one, we are making kime (focusing our power) with the rotation of the hips. So, even though we are turning our hips, we always keep our balance and imagine many opponents around us, not just one.

Kwanku's original master imagined eight opponents. If you can face eight opponents, you can face many more. Before you face your first opponent, you have already decided not to stop until you destroy all of your opponents. This is the original design for Kwanku.

The opening two moves of Kwanku have a very important lesson about breathing. We used to make the kata breathing out with one breath all the way through raising the arms, separating them and bringing them back together again. Now we breathe in during the first move until the arms are at the top. Then as the arms separate, we start breathing out. In this way we draw an opponent in while we inhale but, just before he starts to attack, we exhale strongly with our counterattack, meeting the fullness of our opponent's breathing with a fullness of our own.

In the sixth movement of the kata we straighten our knees, tighten the buttocks and punch immediately. The fist must connect with the whole body and all must be one, not only physically, but mentally as well. This timing must be one. This is one way of making kime.

The shuto strike in movements 16, 21 and 36 is different from the shuto strike in movement 11 of Heian Yodan. We have to make the difference clear. Look at the connection between the hand and the feet in the two katas to study the differences in the moves. In Kwanku we make this strike by rotating the hips strongly and synchronizing the movement of the hips with the movement of the hand. The hip must turn completely. This is the special feature, this particular kime, that the Kwanku experts intended to transmit to us.

After the shuto-uke strikes (in movements 16 and 21), we have a set of movements where we thrust the sword hand forward to the lower level twice (movements 18 to 19 and movements 23 to 24). Master Funakoshi is not clear about the meaning of these movements and for a long time we thought they were all groin attacks. Now we know that the first one in each set is actually a throw against a front kick. After the shuto attack, turn your body to face the front kick. The right hand and arm go out to deflect the kick away from your body. The left hand protects against a simultaneous hand attack to the face and prepares to push against the opponent's upper body. Scoop the right hand under the opponent's kicking leg to lift it and push with the left arm to throw your opponent. Make sure that your right arm ends up in the same line as your body line with the elbow just above shoulder height. The next move is a groin attack, probably against another opponent.

As I mentioned before, the movements where you turn and go down (movements 42 to 45) can be very difficult. Right after you finish the double punch in the movement before (movements 40 and 41) you must feel the opponent behind you. If you don't feel the opponent, you can't make a strong block behind you. So, you feel the opponent. Then as you turn, make sure that the hands go up, passing the thigh and the knee, ending up in front of the chest and face. You are crashing into the opponent's attack and must have the feeling of penetrating him completely. Your body must go in. If you are leaning back, the opponent will push you back instead.

For the next technique (movement 43) drop your body to the ground with either the palms or fingertips resting on the floor. Next turn again to the back and make a lower level block with a sword hand to protect the back knee. Be sure to turn your right foot in at the same time so it is perpendicular to the line of the block. If you don't get your foot turned in, the stance will be weak and the block will be less effective.

Movement 55 is a throw we study in one hand escapes (kata-te-dori).

Tekki (Armed Warrior Riding Horse)

Tekki means armed warrior riding horse, so imagine a solid, powerful and impossible-to-hurt warrior wearing armor and riding a horse into battle. This kind of understanding, practicing a kata to build a really tough, thick and masculine body is an influence from the Shokei style.

Stories say that the Tekki katas date back six or seven centuries, but I really don't know for sure. Originally the three Tekki forms were almost like one continuous form. Some years ago, before Master Funakoshi's period, they were reorganized and separated into Shodan, Nidan and Sandan.

The most important point in Tekki katas is the strong stance with stable hips. These katas are designed to help us understand that kibadachi is the strongest stance that human beings can make — not only solid and powerful and heavy, but also light, movable and quick. When you practice kibadachi, one sensation is that you are very heavy. Nobody can push you out of your stance. At the same time you should not be so heavy that you cannot move quickly. In other words, your feeling is solid but you can still move very easily. Two sensations in one stance: it sounds crazy, but you can make it someday.

To me, kibadachi is the easiest way to understand how all of our techniques connect with every part of the body, standing legs, feet, ankles, and especially the rear leg and rear foot. To make a strong kibadachi means to make our whole body and mind, from bottom to top, as one. We recognize our whole existence as one, feel as one and express ourselves as one. Therefore, in these katas, even the simple stance of kibadachi is important. It's difficult to make a good kibadachi and it takes a lifetime to study how this stance applies in combat or how to connect the blocks, how to connect the attacks, how to use this stance in front of an opponent.

When you practice the Tekki katas, concentrate on making a strong stance with no conscious power in the shoulders or upper body. The head position is very natural with no tension in the neck and shoulders, while your underarms and hips are directly connected to your stance. The elbows never go outside of the body's line. This line changes, depending on how you are facing the opponent. When you face to the front, your body's line is the two lines from the sides of your body to the opponent, and the elbow is always on the line. When you face an opponent to the side, the line is very narrow, but try to get your elbow into that line.

Tekki forms were Master Funakoshi's first training katas. He practiced them for ten years, nothing else but Tekki practice for ten years, more than 30 times every day. That means over 100,000 Tekki katas and beyond that he also did all kinds of kibadachi practices to help polish them. I remember hearing that Master Funakoshi went to Master Anko Itosu's residence at midnight to practice and came home in the early morning hours every day. To visualize Master Funakoshi's Tekki forms we must practice these katas many times. Shotokan members believe there is a special meaning in practicing kibadachi stance and techniques from these katas. Everyone, even white belts, should learn Tekki forms.

Tekki Shodan

Tekki Shodan is one of the best katas, one of the key katas for Shotokan. I consider it to be one of the few complete katas. Even though it doesn't look really fancy, we should practice it as much as we can.

I know most beginners think this kata is very strange, with funny movements, but after I made it about 50,000 times, I understood that this is an exceptionally genuine and honest kata. It may look short and simple, but it's very deep, very remarkable, with many important elements.

It takes more than 10,000 katas before we begin to understand and eliminate our weak points and misunderstandings. With less than that, it looks horrible. Then each 5,000 times you will find some new discovery. So don't form your opinion about this kata after a few hundred or a few thousand times. Only after years of practice does this kata come out naturally from inside.

I don't recommend Tekki Shodan as a favorite form for members taking the shodan test. I encourage you to practice Tekki Shodan (especially to prepare for special training) but for the shodan test you should always select one of the Heian katas for your favorite. Although it may look good to you, your weak points are obvious to someone who has made 50,000 katas. I have seen a few people pass 50,000 times and their Tekki looks really good. In my case even 20,000 times didn't make much of a difference. After another 20,000 times, I started to understand many important elements. Therefore, please don't pick Tekki Shodan as your favorite kata for grading unless you plan to practice it 10,000 to 20,000 times. It's very difficult to get the good points of this form.

In Tekki Shodan, one of the lessons is how to use kibadachi after blocking, at the moment you execute a counterattack or as soon as the opponent starts to attack. For example, at the moment you execute your counterattack, make a strong, low stance. If you let your back heel come up, the technique will only work half way. The punch or kick has to completely connect with your back leg and hips the moment you execute it.

According to the old pictures, the Tekki Shodan stance used to be much narrower. This was to protect the centerline, especially the groin area. As karate went from Okinawa to Tokyo, the stance got a little wider from kendo influences. Because of the beautiful training floors, the preference was to jump in or jump out like a Shaolin movement. In the 1950s it became much wider. Now in the 1990s, we are making the stance narrower again to be ready for a kicking attack from the front, but the original stance was narrower still.

There are a few more points that I want to make about some of the moves in this kata. Before the first movement you must already feel three opponents, one to the left, one to the right and one in front of you. When you start, your mind moves first toward the opponent on your right and your eyes follow. If your mind does not move first, you can injure your body. As you move, put the weight on your right foot, lower your hips and place the left foot just on the other side of the right foot with the toes or the outside edge of the foot lightly touching the floor. The legs are connected to make a solid stance.

When you move in this kata, don't let your hips or head go up and down. Once you go down for the first time, the hips and head stay down at that level and only move in a horizontal direction to the left and right.

When you execute uraken to the front (movements 11 and 29), your fist should stop in front of your mouth. You are attacking your opponent's nose, the chin or even the chest, while standing in kibadachi.

The last move at the end of each half of the kata (movements 19 and 37) is a double punch. You can think of it with either arm attacking. If the forward arm is attacking, then the rear arm may be guarding the chest, blocking or pulling your opponent's arm. If the rear arm attacks, the front arm may be gedan barai. Remember that your opponent is very close.

When you make the kata, don't hurry. Execute each move one by one, exactly. Speed does not come from eliminating movements, it comes from training and a strong mentality. Eventually you can reach a certain level with no conscious power in your shoulders, using your strong willpower with subconscious mental power.

Never overlook your own mistakes, but look at your weaknesses with strong eyes. We are training to try to face ourselves straight, strict and honest. This kata is quite good practice for that.

I think Tekki Shodan brings you some extra energy from deep inside. Always believe in that original energy that you bring up to the higher level of the mind. That's the message for Tekki Shodan.

Tekki Nidan

Just like the other Tekki katas, the fundamental point of Tekki Nidan is the stance. Even though the feeling and movement are different, the stance itself is always strong, powerful and heavy, yet light when moving. The hips have to be free, never locked, and you must connect the upper and lower body movements in the hips.

Tekki Nidan is a very short kata, so don't go too quickly everywhere. You must try to find the rhythm of the kata instead. When you have to move quickly, move quickly with one motion. But when you move more slowly, take your time and don't hurry, especially when you stand up and put both fists under your nipples.

The kibadachi and other basic things are the same as Tekki Shodan. I think somebody who makes Tekki Shodan well shouldn't have any problem with Tekki Nidan. Especially, if you make a good stance, the rest of this practice is just a matter of numbers, maybe a few thousand times.

Tekki Sandan

Tekki Sandan has many arm movements, yet the important point is still the stance itself, so make a solid, strong stance. Everybody should know the correct distance between the two feet, not too wide, not too close. You must be very stable and yet able to move very quickly and very smoothly.

In the third movement, as the right hand blocks across the body to the left, the left fist moves up to the right elbow so as to block a body blow. At this point the forearms are horizontal across the body with the right arm on top. The left hand remains in this position for the next two movements.

Movements 14, 15 and 16 are like the similar movements in Tekki Shodan and Nidan. This series of movements should be like the second and third movements of Heian Sandan (the udeuke and gedan barai combinations). After the left hand udeuke (movement 15) raise the left hand directly up and back and execute a backfist attack (movement 16). These movements should be fast with no appreciable stop between the udeuke and the backfist.

After you make a solid stance with solid hips, your arms are quite free from conscious tension. You should not tense your muscles all the time, and most of the time there is no power. Make the fist with the small finger tight, with the correct position of the elbow, never opening up from the body's line, and the shoulder never going up. When you execute uraken, for instance, use only your subconscious power with your breathing. You don't have to use any power consciously.

Hangetsu (Half Moon)

Hangetsu comes from the Japanese words "Han" which means half and "getsu" which means moon. Your steps are supposed to make a half-moon curve.

Master Funakoshi wrote that Hangetsu comes from the Seisan form, but Hangetsu is completely different and I could not find any similar points with the ancient Seisan kata after I researched both katas. I still respect this kata as Master Funakoshi's Hangetsu.

Hangetsu is a very doubtful kata. It is one of the most mistransmitted katas from senior to junior in Shotokan, and it's very difficult to find this order in any of the ancient forms of the kata. After my study of Hangetsu, I think the stance transmitted to me was exaggerated and opened the centerline too much to the opponent. Originally there was a much narrower stance. We should go back to the original to make a realistic stance which hides your vital points and still lets you make effective kicks or hand techniques.

In Hangetsu stance, we emphasize a very strong back leg. The heel is straight back and the toes face straight toward the opponent. Make your heel always stay solidly on the ground, with the hips never behind the heel. The front knee has to hide your centerline so that you don't get an opponent's front kick directly to the groin. Don't make a kibadachi stance. We have to make it clear that Hangetsu stance has returned to the original Seisan stance. (But we can't go back to the original Seisan Hangetsu, because the order of Master Funakoshi's Hangetsu is completely different.) I have no doubt about the stance itself because it is the only way we can make ideal kime (focus of power) when attacking, blocking or kicking the opponent.

To make a strong stance, almost like immovable stance, don't show any weakness against the opponent's kicks. Never open your centerline to the opponent, no matter what the situation, because the opponent can easily kick your weakest points. When making the Hangetsu stance, the knees are close to protect the centerline, yet they have to be strong against stamping and side thrust kicks. While the knees push outward, the feet push inward to make the knees very strong in both directions.

As you move, the front leg covers your groin and the centerline of the lower part of the body. While you are moving, you actually defend the middle of your body with your own muscle, and your hands only cover your upper body. This kata will develop the muscles in the middle of the body so they will be strong enough to protect you.

Keep the back foot on the ground. Make your stance solid and tall and face straight toward the opponent. This way your gyakuzuki connects to the back heel. If your toes are out, power escapes to the back.

Also, shoulders are completely in and face the front. Don't pull the shoulders back and pinch your shoulder blades together. The back shoulder blade is in, underarms and fists are connected, and both underarms are tight. The meaning of these slow motion blocks and attacks is to develop the underarm muscles and also to make a habit of never letting the elbows stick out.

This kata is very good training for developing strength, especially the very powerful, slow movements of the kata: first to make clear the significant meaning of breathing; second to develop the muscles. Therefore when you do udeuke and then gyakuzuki, keep your elbows in and keep both underarms tight to develop underarm muscles.

Remember to always push your hips in, in front of the back heel. Against pushing power this is really strong. And make your breathing very solid and come to your fingertips so that your fingers become very powerful. These are very important points to develop for the realistic, strong fighter. Young people, especially, should practice this kata a lot to develop the muscles and the body and the breathing.

When practicing Hangetsu, focus on the stances in the kata. Make a strong separation between slowness and quickness. A more excited and immature mentality will make the slow moves quicker than they should.

Jutte (Ten Hands)

Jutte means ten hands. Jutte is a short kata designed with only blocks. There are no attacking techniques unless we consider blocks that are attacks at the same time. This kata is the best practice for blocks. Somebody who can do Jutte very well understands the uke (blocks) of karate and can block any opponent's attack as if he had ten hands.

There are many incomplete parts in the set of katas we study, however, Jutte is one of the few katas that doesn't have many mistakes. Even though it doesn't look fancy, it's a very solid, very correct kata, with all the important movements of blocking.

Starting with the blocks and ending with the blocks, this is, in a way, a beautiful kata and a very ideal kata for the karate practitioner. Originally, in karate practice we started with the blocks. We did not learn how to punch, how to kick, we only learned how to block. Those instructors thought that we should not harm other people, but just protect ourselves. It was the same when I started to practice. The understanding was that if somebody learned how to block perfectly, he was the winner. Originally, karate blocks meant not only protecting yourself from an opponent's attack, but also destroying the opponent with strong blocks when they decide to come destroy you. Therefore, in karate, blocks can sometimes be interpreted as connecting to attacks.

All blocks can, themselves, destroy an opponent. We can learn from this kata that blocks do not mean mechanical movements of the arm or shoulder or body. Blocks mean the whole body follows a strong mind and, as one, we use the block to stop or evade or escape or destroy the opponent's attack as soon as the opponent decides to come attack. We block with the whole body, top to bottom, and the mind. We move with no conscious power and then explode just as we block.

We also consider form, because form itself is strength. Always connect your arms with your hips through the underarms. Elbows never stick out from the lines between the edges of your body and the edges of your opponent's body. Your elbow should be just inside of this line of the bodies or the block won't work.

When you make this kata, there is no moment with the underarm open, the elbows going out, power going up to the shoulders, eyes looking down or hips getting weaker ... there is no such moment. So, you have to make this form with strong, low hips, underarms always slightly tight, and elbows, even when hands go up, still connected with both underarms.

Master Funakoshi wrote in his book slow and fast, expand and contract, power and no power and, of course, we have these three elements, but there is something more we have to find. There is mental speed, mental rhythm. Rhythm leads our understanding. If somebody doesn't understand, doesn't get the rhythm, they really can't understand this kata. The rhythm that we have comes from our seniors, masters and the geniuses who polished the kata for many centuries and passed it down to us. It is important to look for the correct speed and rhythm.

When you are young and immature, anything quick is fancy and charming, but speed is not the absolute objective. Speed is very subjective. Speed is the relationship between you and your particular opponent. Don't go too quickly in every part. Quick movements exist because there are slow movements.

In a real situation, how do you pull your opponent to your rhythm? By your mental strength, your mental level. Therefore when you practice katas, always face yourself and find your own best rhythm, your own best speed. When you make it quick, be quick; when you have to make it slowly, take your time. Some young people, however, want to make every movement quickly, and make the katas in such a hurry that they make a mistake. There are two things you don't have to do quickly: don't make your life short and don't make a mistake fast. A mistake is okay, but the feeling of haste is one of the weakest expressions.

Everyone should be able to practice this kata and learn that effective blocks come from a strong stance. We have to make solid, precise stances (zenkutsu, kokutsu, kibadachi and heisoku-dachi). And remember in hand techniques not to stiffen or tense your arm muscles. Momentarily, we use strength, but most of the time there is no conscious power in the shoulders or arms.

Originally, the starting form of the two hands meant sun and moon. The right hand is the sun and the left is the crescent moon. One technique to study is the third movement. When the left hand goes down to the horizontal and you face to your right, at this moment your hips have to turn for this pushing down block and in preparation for the next right hand udeuke with teisho. There is no explanation of this movement of the left hip in the book, but without the hips you cannot block the other direction.

Senior members have to learn another point in this kata called yamagamae, or mountain posture (in movements 10 to 13). This form doesn't work if your elbow is even a little bit lower or higher than the shoulder. Your elbows have to be exactly shoulder level and also exactly to the sides. Be careful not to use any conscious power in your shoulders, keep your underarms slightly tight and never lock your shoulder blades together in the middle of the back. Without the correct form, this block will never be effective. Therefore, you must practice with a friend and test this block so that you can find out how to make it effective and realistic, and to understand that when your arms come up without conscious power you can still block against an opponent's strong attack.

Also, many people are forgetting that the turning of the head in Jutte is one technique. Especially when you are facing straight, the moment your opponent starts to attack, suddenly turn your head to the left or right. When you turn to face him suddenly this way, he hesitates. Your sudden motion freezes him momentarily so make these motions clearly, precisely.

To understand the moves necessary to stop an opponent's bo (rod or stick) attack in movements 15 to 18, you have to practice with your friends. This way you can discover how the bo moves when you are attacked and how you have to grasp it, turn your wrist, take the bo with the opponent's pushing power and then counterattack with the bo. I hope everybody enjoys practicing with the bo.

In the last few moves starting with movement 21, after throwing to the right and then to the left side, we straighten the knees with the right open-hand ageuke and tighten the buttocks. Then hook the opponent's arm and step directly forward with a left ageuke.

Empi (Flying Swallow)

Empi means flying swallow or swallow flight. ("Em" means swallow and "pi" means flying.) This kata has quite fancy techniques and many dynamic hip movements. Without these dynamic hip movements, we cannot make a beautiful and effective Empi.

I'm sure young men and women who feel very light and who can jump in very deeply and turn beautifully with one-motion hip movements, will enjoy this kata, facing many opponents, especially to the front and back. I hope everyone under 40 years old really enjoys it. Even after 40, although you cannot jump that much, you can still enjoy a free, light and dynamic feeling. Warm up well so you don't hurt your tendons.

You should be careful to avoid the feeling that you want to show off or exaggerate some parts. Your attention instead should go to your hip movement. Without dynamic hip motions, this kata is dead. You have to be very humble and keep a realistic sense of combat, executing each technique seriously, instead of just trying to make them look fancy.

I hope that somebody who practices Empi makes it 5,000 times and then goes on to 10,000 times. Somebody who is really trying to make Empi as a favorite kata, should do it at least 20,000 times. Then this kata will begin to show some of its original feeling, and you will start to feel what the original master was trying to tell us through the kata.

Many people have asked about the first movements of Empi. This is a throwing technique. The opponent is coming from the right side. You block his arm with your left arm and sweep the opponent's front leg or back leg with your right arm. The moment when you turn is very quick and with one feeling. Don't create your own rhythm. We are seeking to understand the mind, feeling and movements of the expert who invented the kata.

The third movement is gedan barai with the right arm in zenkutsu like the third movement of Heian Shodan. Then in movement 4 straighten both knees simultaneously with a left handed kagizuki (cross-body punch) and face to the front.

The uraken in Empi (in movements 6, 10 and 26) is a swinging attack. The uppercut under the chin of the opponent doesn't work without rotating the hips. Practice the technique lightly, with no conscious power, and be sure to make the connection with your hip.

Another important point is not to cut in half the series of movements beginning with the knee coming up. (These are movements 7-9, 11-13 and 27-29.) Raise the knee, jump in and attack the lower part of the opponent's abdomen, then kokutsu and gedan barai with the right arm, and then turn around with zenkutsu and make gedan barai with the left hand. This is all made with one breath, with no stop in between. In this quick sequence the hips almost never stop moving. The most difficult parts, I think, are to get in to the front and then turn around and block, with both blocks as one feeling. Actually, your hips are making dynamic movements, making an effective block on one side and then the other without any break between the two techniques. This is difficult, but if you try, your hips will start to move. Like the flight of a swallow, this turning has to be very quick.

Empi is good for the younger generation because they don't use jumping in techniques enough. The tobikomi techniques (movements 7, 11 and 27) are disappearing in competition because competition has very limited space and you cannot jump in very far. People have forgotten how to jump in. But if you use tobikomi techniques in a very big place, they are safe and very effective. So emphasize the jump using your back leg to get into the opponent. Remember that your hips do not go up. The knee goes up, but the hips go down, and you hide your whole middle section.

When you jump in, put the knees together to act as a brake, stopping suddenly, with the knees and hips level, parallel to the floor. The hips never go lower than the knees and the left toes lightly touch the right heel on the right side. If the hips are too high, you cannot stop dynamically. If the hips go lower than the knees, the knees will be injured.

When you make teisho-uke (movements 30-33), both elbows are bent, unlocked. After the first teisho-uke with the right hand (movement 30), step to the front with the right leg, without moving the left leg.

After the third morote-uke (the two-handed blocks, one upward and one downward with teisho in movements 31-33), make gedan barai in kokutsu (movement 34). Then yoriashi (in movement 35) with both hands open, right elbow against the side, palm up and left forearm about nine inches from the forehead slightly above the head with the left palm up. The feeling is to grab the arm or neck with the left hand and the shin or crotch with the right hand.

Don't make this kata too quickly. In the last twenty years (1970 to 1990), everybody has almost doubled the speed of this kata. I like to see young people make very quick movements in the kata, but you have to take your time, be calm and show a big, strong feeling. Especially right after the kiai (movement 15), there is just a little pause in the movement. There are many good techniques here, therefore, I'm sure you can pick some of your favorite techniques from this kata.

Gankaku (Crane on a Rock)

Gankaku means crane on a rock. ("Gan" means rock and "kaku" means crane.) The form where we stand on one leg is the reason for the name. There is no historical data on Gankaku. It is not as old as Heian Shodan or Tekki Shodan and not as new as Kwanku, so it originated somewhere between 300 and 1,000 years ago. Maybe in the future we will find some books to study about the background of this kata but, as far as I know, the origin of this kata is quite unknown.

I think the person who invented this kata was quite tall, with long arms and long legs. Maybe this person was around 30 to 45 years old, but not older than that. And not much younger, because the kata is quite refined and the understanding is terrific. He had quite a good understanding of kime (focusing his power) and also knew how to keep his balance while moving. Even though this is a one-line kata, Gankaku is genuine, realistic and beautiful.

Gankaku *is* a one-line kata so be cautious with your movements. Many people are making many lines here: big, thick lines or two or three lines. We have to make exact steps and keep our body and stance always on one line. By the line, I don't mean the thin line a sharp pencil makes on paper. I mean the body's thickness, about a ten-inch-wide line. Along the line you must practice to find an extensive feeling.

When you turn, for instance, with kibadachi, make kibadachi on the line. Don't step forward or backward. When you make the turning motions, always turn with the hip, without allowing any weak points or losing your balance. This is a matter of hip movements, not steps.

After you execute this kata many times, and it's becoming your favorite, you can make each movement quicker. This kata has very slow, medium and very quick speeds. Showing the slow and quick movements, and the extension and contraction, based on the feeling, rhythm and breathing of the kata, is what gives it life. Make slow and quick movements clearly, yet don't cut the kata into two or three parts. It is one form with many elements.

Young people can do this kata very quickly, but after a certain age it is kind of hard to keep your balance while standing on one leg. This is a very good kata to concentrate your mind, yet your body is very free to move with any kind of stance. Although Gankaku gives the impression of up and down movements, your hips are almost always stabilized and solid, and you never lose your balance against opponents.

Gankaku has many blocks against kicking attacks. Although it is not really indicated, when we make gedan barai, actually we are crushing the opponent's toes, ankles or shin as part of the counterattack. When you make gedan barai with the right or left hand, you must execute it very strongly. Many people are missing this part these days.

Gankaku also shows kibadachi gyakuzuki, one of the most effective thrusts (movements 32 and 36). I think Master Funakoshi got gyakuzuki from this kata. Make sure you make this punch from a good kibadachi.

The standing and turning on one leg (movement 40) is difficult to do without hurting the knee. Therefore, when you turn with one leg, be careful not to hurt your knee. I think in the beginning they did not turn with one leg, but with two legs, and that later some unrealistic people eliminated turning with two legs for some theatrical effect or for the sense of beauty of standing on one leg. Yet, if you turn with one leg many thousands of times, eventually you start to hurt your knee. Therefore, you have to be careful.

For the young man or woman without any knee problems, you shouldn't lose your balance and strength when turning on one leg. But if you have knee problems, don't risk hurting your own knee. Find ways to turn with two legs safely. When you turn, keep a strong standing leg and don't let the knee be weak from the side. Everybody has to know what that is. I suggest turning with two legs and then going up onto one leg.

Balance is important, especially with the last uraken and yokogeri keage and then oizuki (movements 41 and 42), if your feeling and your hips go up, power goes to your shoulders, the punch connects to the shoulders and your oizuki is not right. So be aware of your tanden (the lower part of the abdomen) making yokogeri keage, uraken and oizuki with your hips and kiai. This makes this kata look beautiful.

When we practice a kata, not just a few thousand times, but more than ten thousand times, we have to be very careful to avoid movements that hurt the body. If you are hurting your body, you are doing something wrong. In this case, it's the turning parts that can damage the knees. We are practicing a lifetime so we have to be aware of these weak points to avoid injury.

Jion

Jion is a relatively new kata that came out of the Okinawan Islands, according to what we know now, in 1663 or 1680. This is in the same period as Kwanku.

There is a temple and a Buddhist priest who were named Jion. I read once in a history book that there was even a bridge named Jion Bridge. We don't know exactly from which this kata gets its name. I suppose that some Okinawan people around that time liked the name Jion. One legend is that the inventor of the kata practiced on the Jion Bridge and that was how the kata received its name.

In Jion, two schools, Shaolin and Shokei, meet to make one kata. Shaolin is a light, quick style. Shokei is the name of the heavy, powerful school. I hope that some of you who pick this kata as a favorite will practice it until you are satisfied that you have made it as one unified kata.

(Just as a note: Shokei is the name that the old experts of karate in the Okinawan Islands used. Many books, even Master Funakoshi's book, **Karate-Do Kyohan** spelled Shokei differently. It was written "Shorei." That is the wrong spelling and also the wrong character. There is no Shorei that existed in the past. Shokei is the exact word and character for this school.)

I think Jion is a very solid kata, quite orthodox, with very few negative elements. It is long and can be difficult but, if you stick with it, you should not have any problems executing it, especially if you can make oizuki clearly. For somebody who cannot make oizuki clearly and realistically, with a simple, clean attack, Jion must be very difficult. There are not many fancy techniques but it is a powerful and strong kata, one of the most refined.

It is one of the very few forms with no contradictory, unhealthy or unclear movements. The kata is very well designed. I haven't found any mistakes, so everybody can practice Jion with a very comfortable feeling that what we are practicing here won't hurt our bodies. Make an exact stance and your stance will lead your technique to the proper way. I really recommend it for people who have problems with knees or legs or arms.

We don't have many difficult points in the interpretation of this kata and I think it is very clear what we are doing in most parts. Therefore, it is very easy to get into the kata and repeat it many times.

There are three parts to this kata, but the punctuation between parts is a semi-colon, not a period. You should never feel that you are stopping between parts; always feel continuously and make it one kata with three parts. Mentally, you have to continue strongly throughout the entire kata. Maintain continuous breathing and feeling. There is no moment to relax. And even though it is very difficult to execute this kata with one concentrated feeling, this is a very good challenge for all black belts, especially nidans who have to make this kata 5,000 times.

The rhythm or tempo of this kata is not always the same. There's quick and slow. Especially when standing and preparing for the next movements, don't go too fast. Take time to prepare your mind and breathing, then continue to execute the form, yet never for a moment allow your concentration and mentality to weaken.

Another important point when we are practicing ageuke-gyakuzuki, ageuke-gyakuzuki, then ageuke-oizuki is that we have to be careful of the position of both shoulders when executing gyakuzuki. Your shoulder line has to be 90 degrees from the direction of your forward movement. And when you execute oizuki, your right shoulder goes to the front, the left shoulder goes back and down and connects with the back heel.

I consider Jion to be one of the most mature forms. It is just a little longer than most, but I hope senior members recognize the value of this form and, as we should try to do with all of the forms, get in this form and get out from this form someday.

Ten No Kata (Form of Heaven)

Ten No Kata means form of heaven. Ten No Kata originally was designed by Master Funakoshi and was demonstrated by his son, Yoshitaka Funakoshi who passed away in 1947 when he was 27 or 28 years old. This was Yoshitaka (also known as Gigo) Funakoshi's favorite practice after he mastered all of the basics. Yoshitaka Sensei was very well-trained, a karate genius and he loved the fudodachi stance.

Ten No Kata was not originally put into **Karate-Do Kyohan** as a kata, but Master Funakoshi's son liked this kata, practicing it and Ten No Kata Ura many times with Master Egami and others. Actually, Ten No Kata is originally the first basic kata, but is referred to as Kumite Kata.

In his book, Master Funakoshi indicates making Ten No Kata with fudodachi (immovable stance). However, I ask all junior members to practice with zenkutsu (front stance) and kokutsu (back stance). There is a reason. After we learn zenkutsu and then kokutsu, we can learn fudodachi without much trouble, but if we practice fudodachi in the beginning, we have difficulty learning zenkutsu. Therefore, I suggest that junior members use zenkutsu stance. It is important to stand mainly with your back leg because the back leg is the strength of the stance. To perform it properly, keep your back toes in, knee straight and hips in. When members reach black belt level, after they have a good back leg and a good strong zenkutsu, then they can learn how to practice with fudodachi. This stance is the cousin of kibadachi, so everybody should be able to figure out how to make it right.

When teaching Ten No Kata, in the beginning, make it precisely, exactly, with a big feeling. Always emphasize a big feeling first. Don't shrink. Second, emphasize a strong feeling; third, quickness; and fourth, lightness, including smooth, fluid movements. Some beginners, especially young people, skip the big, strong feeling — for example, at special training — and get into just the quickness or lightness. They miss something this way, so the first emphasis of this practice, or generally of any practice, should be to make everybody feel big and strong.

All brown belts must begin to understand that the counterattack is not separated from the block. The important point of the movements in Ten No Kata is to show that we understand the block and attack are one connected movement with one feeling and one breathing. There is no space between the block and the attack, so we must always try to make both as one continuous movement. As soon as we block, we are already making our strongest counterattack.

For somebody who really wants to make a simple, solid, realistic counterattack, no matter what kind of opponent comes to attack, and make it with strong spirit and a good sense of distance and timing, this is one of the best practices.

Practicing Kata

There are two opinions given in **Karate-Do Kyohan** about which katas are best and how you should practice katas. One opinion was expressed by my senior, Master Shigeru Egami, who felt that the Taikyoku katas were the ideal form and should be practiced the most. The other opinion is that expressed by Master Gichin Funakoshi. He asked that we pick a form which is most ideal for us and study and practice that form many times. This is difficult without knowing each individual form first. By learning each form in a basic manner, the ideal or favorite form would eventually be found.

In Shotokan, our first year and a half is usually spent learning the Heian katas, then later learning Bassai and Kwanku at brown belt level. After shodan we practice a different kata every month so as to make ourselves familiar with all nineteen forms. In this way the student will know all of the katas and should find which form is best for him.

As we practice, we have to be careful to keep the original form and not make changes in the katas. Even myself, I have a few questions about some parts, but I don't have a chance to ask Master Funakoshi any more, so we have to keep the form exactly as Master wrote in the book. I'm just telling people, don't make changes according to your own level right now. Otherwise the next generation will not know the original movements.

To practice katas, we must always be strict with ourselves. We have to maintain traditional katas precisely. We don't have any right to change or modify or interpret with our own personal viewpoint at our level. We always have to keep a humble mind, because someone trained for many years to try to transmit some important points in the katas. We must transmit these points through the katas.

When we practice a kata many times, we can feel the personality of those who practiced it many years ago, especially the original person who made it. Even though we try to keep the katas the same, certain parts change over many years. Still, we can feel the original master.

Kihon (Basics)

Kihon is the practice of basic techniques, one technique at a time or, maybe, a combination of two or three techniques. It is important, whenever we experience confusion about sophisticated practice, to go back to the practice of basics, for it is in basics that we can find clear answers. No matter what level you reach, you should go back to the basics from time to time.

There are three important points in basics:
- eyes showing a strong mental attitude
- strong stance
- pulling hand.

First is mental attitude. There is a strong connection between our mental attitude and our eyes, so always keep your eyes open and level. Don't look down or blink or turn your head. Get in the habit of looking straight at the opponent all of the time. When you are practicing with other people, especially if you are a senior, don't give the wrong impression and create bad habits by looking down to check your feet or your pulling hand. These are things you can check when you practice by yourself. When you are with juniors, always emphasize keeping strong eyes.

Second, you have to make a strong stance. No matter whether you are blocking or attacking, or whether you are making oizuki or gyakuzuki, the important thing is simultaneous dynamic hip movements. The strongest stances emphasize the rear foot on the ground connected to the hips with a strong back leg.

Third, when you execute a block or attack, you must make a proper pulling hand (hikite) with the hand just above the hip bone. This is important because it develops both sides of the body. Usually, people stand mainly with the front leg and their rear leg is weak. Or they execute their favorite technique with one side but the other side is asleep. Therefore, we always make proper coordination with the pulling hand to remind ourselves that both sides of the body need to work together. If you understand these elements, your techniques will start to be effective because your mind and body movements become one.

As we learn basics there are three stages that each of us need to go through. First we emphasize a big feeling, second power and third speed. First, mind leads, then feeling follows the mind, then the body follows the feeling. What we know is that power and speed and correct form actually come from the feeling. If we start with the form and not the feeling, it is very hard to figure out what to do. So, instead, we work on a big feeling first. Then this big feeling itself seems to pull the body into the right form to make the most powerful techniques. If we start by trying to make good form and skip the feeling, some people never understand the importance of a big feeling in our practice.

Next we start to look at the form of the technique — how to make all the parts work together to make the most powerful basic. Many elements are important, but the most important is the center of our power, our hips. Use your big feeling to make the hips go in each time. When you think of power, think of how to make each technique simultaneously with the hips. The mind, the feeling and the hips have to go together. Along with that you need to connect the other parts of the body to the hips to make exact form. Exact form is important because form itself is strength.

When we start to work on speed, we have to remember that absolute speed is not as important as the feeling of speed between opponents. We don't eliminate parts of the technique and make it weaker to make ourselves faster because then the technique won't work. Instead, we eliminate all of the extra motions and ways we telegraph our intentions through breathing, physical or mental means. Eliminating all of the unnecessary parts is how we learn to make faster techniques. Be especially careful not to move the front foot before starting.

When you study basics don't get in the habit of being sloppy or easily forgiving your mistakes. You must get a strict and strong habit of practice in your mind. The purpose of this strict adherence to precise form is the strong mentality that attention nurtures. Only stronger mentality brings a higher level. I hope all junior members understand that we are going to practice for many years to come. We should not waste time. Your practice should always be strong and effective and realistic, so that some day you can defend yourself against a strong opponent's attack. Our mentality, when we make basics, is that we always imagine an opponent and then ask ourselves, is this realistic and effective or not.

One must have a mature mind and humble manner to see the refined art which took the masters their whole lives to develop. We must have the humility and critical eye to see form precisely. This preciseness is honesty and gives us a way to see ourselves accurately. There are two levels of practice when it comes to preciseness. In level one, when we practice basics, we try to keep our strong and honest mind to look at ourselves and execute techniques as precisely as possible. We are trying to reach the ideal basic. In level two seniors get out from this concern for exact form. Then we become free to express our own feeling and adjust correctly to the situation to make the best technique and our own unique element.

Modern man has many complex philosophical questions and to resolve them it is wise to look at them from the perspective of primitive man. Budo practice gives us a hint that when we are troubled by abstract problems of modern society, we should try to think as we would if we were living in a primitive state. In this way we can find a simpler solution to our problems. This is closely related to karate practice. If we are having problems with our practice, it is good to return to basics.

How to Practice Basics

I would like to discuss *how* we practice basic techniques and *how many* times we should repeat each technique. One thing we have to avoid is the lazy, immature mentality where, after only ten or twenty times, we stop and say to ourselves, okay, that's good enough. That's a really stupid way to practice basics. It doesn't mean anything.

On the other hand we have to avoid being hard-headed and doing more and more repetitions and thinking that, because we are doing so many techniques, that that's great. That is not the way either, because we will lose all of our junior members and there is the risk that we will ruin our health by permanently damaging some part of our body through too much practice.

So it's our responsibility to be aware of this, to be alert and see the human mind, human body, and consider the length of our lives. We have to be healthy and yet very strong, and remember that we are stepping up one by one to reach a higher level.

In special training it's kind of difficult and we repeat, for instance, 100 of each basic technique. Maybe we have 15 basics, that means 1,500 basic techniques. And when we make 100 or 200 of each kick, that means 1,000 kicks. The problems come when people increase the numbers because they're challenging a higher level or trying to make it more difficult. There has to be a balance. If we repeat techniques too many times, we lose our strength and get permanently damaged.

Of course, we have to penetrate our mental blocks and our imagined limitations, but we also have to know that such practices can be bad for our life. From my experience, the worst basic is one we do wrong many times. Therefore, basics have to be very precise and should be healthy and not cause damage. All instructors and senior members have to take responsibility for this.

Our current method of teaching basics — first blocks, then punches, and then kicks — came from the university karate club in Tokyo after the 1920s, and was very new. Before that time, instructors always started with the katas, and the basic practice was just analyzing techniques from katas. Somebody who could not make the first move in Heian Shodan, had to do many gedan barai. That was the way basic training started.

To me, and this is my subjective opinion right now, kicks should be taught first, followed by blocks and then punches. That's my opinion. Of course, you can say kicks and then punches and then blocks. I taught that way in the beginning. This discussion should be continued.

We used to practice all basics a hundred times each in the same way as we make them for shodan test or special training. (That is gedan barai, ageuke, udeuke, tetsui, shuto-uke, oizuki, gyakuzuki, maegeri, mawashigeri, yokogeri keage, yokogeri kekomi, mikazukigeri and fumikomi.) However, if you do a hundred of each basic, it's quite difficult because you have to make many techniques and each technique is not improved much with just a hundred repetitions. And if you do it the same way but with fewer numbers, say twenty or forty of each block and punch and kick, then it takes a long time to improve each technique.

I think we should emphasize one particular technique at least 200 to 500 times in each practice and save the other techniques for other practices. Over the last few years I have tried teaching maegeri this way. When we kick maegeri 500 times, even beginners can learn front kick within a few months. During this time, perhaps we cannot teach side thrust kick or roundhouse kick or fumikomi, but we can teach side up kick.

For instance, we can practice five or six different ways to make front kick: standing with both feet together; from front stance, alternate kicking and stepping back and then kicking; marching kick, up and down the floor; continuous kicks, five to ten times; and then side up kick with the same set of exercises. Then we can add at the end of these kicks jumping-in front kick or side up kick, or maybe kick with hand techniques.

We can create many different ways to kick so that, even if we kick 400 to 500 times, we never get tired mentally or emotionally and can still put our energy into basic practice. This way our kicks will improve much more quickly.

For the beginner it's much easier to train with kicks because everybody has strong legs and can kick many times (at least 200). Beginners don't have to kick 1,000 times every day, because they don't know how to kick right yet. But after you learn to kick correctly, there is nothing wrong with kicking about 500 times a day.

When you kick 500 times, you should do less of other techniques. You don't have to do everything. For instance, just include one block or one punch. That's enough.

Then the next month, maybe we emphasize just one block. Take tetsui or udeuke, for example. You could do a couple hundred udeuke, first to the side and then stepping forwards, and then maybe udeuke-gyakuzuki combinations. This way, you make 400 to 500 udeuke and your udeuke improves a lot.

Tetsui takes even less time to learn when we make the same variety, stepping forward, back or in combinations. Execute the same block many times in different ways and you will be able to do it within a very short time. With this practice tetsui becomes very powerful within a few weeks. This way, when you work on other techniques, it will be much easier to reach the same levels.

Sometimes I emphasize five or six techniques (as in August 1994 when the basic practice was maegeri, mawashigeri, mikazukigeri, uraken and gyakuzuki) so you can do them 200 times each or 1,000 times in all. Sometimes we can do that much. When you are doing a set of techniques like these, try to challenge basics and make all of them in about 30 minutes, non-stop. Everybody should have the stamina to make 1,000 techniques that way. This is not every month, but sometimes it is a good idea.

Zenkutsu Dachi (Front Stance)

Zenkutsu dachi means front stance. Many people mistakenly think that front stance means only "bend the front leg" stance. Actually, the back leg supports the hips and body. The front leg is bent and not resisting so that one may move forward easily. Check your back leg so that the toe is not turned out of the body's line, the edge of the foot is not up and the heel is not up. The feet are at shoulder width. The back knee is straight but not locked. Don't lean over or back.

I always emphasize standing mainly by the back leg. Don't put all your weight on the front leg and have a weak back one. Correct the way you use the back leg in front stance so that even if an opponent sweeps the front leg, you don't fall down.

Instructors have to be sure that all members are strict and keep low hips, even though this basic training is much harder. Some schools like Shotokai, where Master Egami led, or others in south China, taught this extremely low stance, with hips at knee level. The reason is that, in a real fight, everybody's feeling automatically goes up. When we make contact with the opponent's body, the height of the hips is the key to keeping our balance, so we want our hips lower than our opponent's. This is why we have to always practice as low as possible and anticipate that we are going to come up a little bit in real time. Keeping low hips also brings your most courageous feeling from the bottom of your mind.

Zenkutsu for beginners should be practiced with the hips at knee level, but not lower because the stance becomes weak if the hips are lower than that. Of course, we understand that at the highest level we can be free from any such restrictions, but this is at a much later stage.

I don't teach fudodachi before I teach zenkutsu because if beginners don't learn how to make a solid zenkutsu first, with a strong back leg and strong supporting hips, they will have much more difficulty learning zenkutsu later on.

Kokutsu Dachi (Back Stance)

Kokutsu dachi means back stance. When you make kokutsu, stand with the weight on the back leg with the hips just a little ahead of, never behind, the rear heel. Bend your rear knee and turn the toes of your back foot so they are in front of the heel. Never let your toes point away from your opponent. Don't shift the weight to the outside of the rear foot with the big toe up in the air. Put the weight evenly on all parts of your foot. Tighten the muscles on the inside of the thigh to make a solid back stance.

Kokutsu has only two conditions.

First your front leg has to be free of your weight and not required for your balance. In other words, if your opponent sweeps at your front leg, you won't fall down. You should be able to easily lift the foot out of the way to escape from the opponent's sweep and then be able to execute maegeri. No matter how strong or how good an athlete you are, if you cannot make back stance right, you could be the victim of a throwing technique. No matter how the opponent tries to sweep your front leg, with a good back stance you should not fall down.

Second you must stand strongly with the back leg and be able to resist the pushing power of an opponent in front of you. Even though your front leg is free and you are standing on the back leg, you must still be able to resist a charging opponent. When your weight is shifted too far back or your head or hips are behind your rear heel, you will be pushed over by the opponent. The hip is just a little bit in front of the heel. Your back heel has to be very strong and your toes have to go in to make kokutsu against the pushing power of your opponent. Also, don't open your knees by standing with the feet too far outside your line toward the opponent, and don't cross the position of the front and back foot. The front and back foot are just a little outside of the line toward the opponent.

This practice takes years and years. Even seniors must continue to practice: back leg, back ankle, strong back foot, heel always on the ground and hips never too far forward or too far back.

I expect that everybody will practice kokutsu dachi in combination with strong hand techniques such as shuto-uke or nukite. The feeling has to come to the fingertips, because it's easy to hurt your fingers. The block is made with the elbow and underarm, the whole body, with the form and fingers connected with the back leg.

I suggest that instructors, when teaching kokutsu, first teach how to make the basic hand and hip movements. Then have beginners practice jumping back at a 45 degree angle into kokutsu and blocking, first to the left and then to the right. When you jump and land with the back foot, keep the rear toes in and make a strong rear leg. Practicing kokutsu moving forwards comes later. Beginners should just practice stepping back.

Later you can make a front leg kick immediately after you land. That way people start to understand that we are standing with the rear leg and the front leg has to be free to kick the opponent as we land. Everyone should realize that to stand with one leg and make a kick is very difficult against a bigger, tougher opponent. There are two important points. First, you have to execute the right timing. The moment your opponent starts to come, you start to kick. Second, your standing leg has to be solid, because you must keep your balance while supporting not only your weight but also your opponent's weight, momentum and power. This takes a strong standing leg. With this practice kokutsu will become a realistic back stance and our basic stance will be improved.

Kibadachi (Horse Riding Stance)

Kibadachi means horse riding stance. It is a tradition of Shotokan that kibadachi was Master Funakoshi's favorite stance. And then, many years after I started practice, I recognized it as the strongest stance that human beings can make. It is the easiest way to understand how all of the techniques connect with every part of the body. To make a strong kibadachi means to make our whole body and mind, from bottom to top, as one. In other words, we recognize our whole existence as one, feel as one and express ourselves as one.

Kibadachi is not only solid and powerful and heavy, but also light, mobile and quick. You can move to the front or back, advance and retreat, even move to the side, without any problems, without losing your balance and always keeping your focus of strength and power toward your opponent. It is the easiest stance for making kime (your strongest focus to the opponent).

When we make special training, one of the treasures of our practice is our one hour and a half in kibadachi stance. Only people who have had the experience of standing in kibadachi many times in special training can find out what kibadachi stance really means and discover the ideal stance and mentality in front of opponents. Not only do we learn how to stand, but also how to look at ourselves with a strong mentality. I'm sure that most members who have attended special training still remember how to stand in kibadachi for an hour and a half.

We make kibadachi by bending both knees with the feet parallel and making a squeezing feeling between the legs, much like holding on with the legs to ride a horse bareback. To check the distance between the feet in a kibadachi stance, lower one knee toward the other foot. The knee should be about two fists distance from the foot. When you bring the kneeling leg back up, your feet will be at the proper distance. Keep your feet flat on the floor, lift the toes off the floor and then set them down so they touch the floor lightly. Don't grip the floor with your toes. The knees are in the straight line between the eyes and the toes. Don't raise the inside of the feet. Keep the feet flat. Keep a strong rear end, squeeze the buttocks toward the front, but don't push your hips forward and stretch the groin muscles. Keep the upper body straight up over the hips. Relax the shoulders. Don't curl the body forward over the solar plexus and let the hips go back.

The feeling you are looking for has three parts. The upper body feeling goes down into the tanden (lower abdomen) and all the feeling goes toward the ground. The feeling in the legs and feet goes in and up, as if standing on a big, round ball, connecting the legs so that even if somebody sweeps one of your legs, you won't fall down. Both feelings meet and are combined at the tanden.

To check the height of the stance and the hips position, jump into the air, pull your knees to your chest and land softly in kibadachi again. Your body weight will put your hips in the right position when you land. Now jump up and make a 180 degree turn in the air before you land. Did you go down before you made the jump? Then your kibadachi started too high. You should be able to jump without going down first.

To study moving to the side in kibadachi, look to your right. Quickly move to the right and as soon as you land move back to the left to your original position. Do this until you can get in and out very quickly, almost as fast as you can make two claps with your hands. Of course you also make this movement facing to the left and you can practice going back first and then in. If you have trouble making this move quickly, there are two points to check. First, your feet must be in the proper position, exactly parallel and perpendicular to your line of movement. You cannot move quickly if your toes point out. Second, your hips must always stay at the same height. Not only does this make you faster, it also makes it more difficult for your opponent to see your movements.

The recent form of kibadachi is a bit wider than when Master Funakoshi first learned it. At that time, kibadachi was not as wide, but narrower with higher hips. The main reason for this change is that when karate went to Tokyo, it was practiced in kendo dojos instead of on the Okinawan terrain which is covered with volcanic rocks. Compared to that a kendo dojo is a huge place where you can easily move around a lot.

When you make kibadachi to the side, it is one of the strongest stances you can make. The only disadvantage is that it's easy for your opponent to attack you with a kick to your front knee, front thigh or groin.

Kibadachi and punches:

Kibadachi does not exist by itself. Kibadachi with an attack, kibadachi with a block — we must think of realistic applications with this stance.

The first practice begins from natural stance. Move one leg to the side and attack with a punch to the side from a strong kibadachi stance with toes in, heels out and bent knees. Keep your balance with your upper body on the line directly to the side. When you execute a punch with the front fist, make it straight, shoulder height, with both shoulders on the line of the stance. Alternate with attacks to the right and left. You can shift your stance or slide your stance and still simultaneously execute your kibadachi-zuki.

The next practice is to step to the front in kibadachi with each punch. This time your hip movement increases the effectiveness of your fist. Therefore, move your hips dynamically, simultaneously executing your punch. When you step in with the right leg and attack with the right fist, don't move your foot out of the line of the movement. Instead, move the right foot toward the center, turn the hips quickly to put the right hip forward, exposing the centerline as little as possible and step out again in a straight line ending up in kibadachi. Don't open your centerline and always go straight toward the power of your opponent. When you begin to shift your hips with your fist, your power goes to the opponent and this technique becomes very powerful. Remember your pulling underarm, pulling hand and, especially, to keep your back toes in and heels out.

After you get used to this move and can do it quickly, you can practice stepping back from natural stance to evade an opponent's attack and then thrust. When you step back, do it the same way as you step to the front. Don't step straight back by moving your foot out of the line of motion. Instead, move your foot inward to the centerline as the initial move of the step. This is much quicker. Even though you are stepping back, the hip movement is not just to the back. As soon as your standing foot is in place, your hips have to shift to the front with your fist to make an effective counterattack. If your fist goes one direction and your hips go the opposite direction, your counterattack will never work.

I am very surprised that karate practitioners here and in Japan don't use this technique more. It is very effective and realistic. I would always have friends from Japan ask me why this technique is so effective. So, I had to show them lightly by making contact with their stomach. All

Shotokan members should practice these techniques a lot and make them their basic secret weapon.

We do not practice punching to the front from kibadachi any more, especially from a wide kibadachi. When you are facing straight ahead, your entire centerline is open to the opponent and neither attacking hand has any kime (way to focus power). [For suggestions about punching to the front from similar stances, see the discussion on bari-bari.]

Kibadachi In Kihon:

We can practice kihon making all of the movements with kibadachi. This is the bridge to real combat, when we can move freely, naturally, lightly, yet we have the strength of kibadachi in every moment when we execute techniques, blocks or attacks or kicks. [See the discussion of kibadachi-zuki in the section on fist attacks.]

Kibadachi In Kumite:

We also make kumite using kibadachi. This is to learn how to move in kibadachi against a real opponent. After many thousands of times we start to understand how we can be a strong human being, as one, with this strong stance. One application that we make is to punch from kibadachi with a higher stance, like a boxer executing a jab with kibadachi.

Kibadachi At Special Training:

People coming back from special training know how difficult it is to stand in kibadachi correctly for an hour and a half. I think that all members who attend special training and practice kibadachi begin wondering, "What is this stance?" By standing for a long time, not only do you learn to develop a strong will, but you also learn how to make a better stance. Your body unconsciously learns how to stand economically and strongly without thinking.

I'm sure most junior members who go to special training suffer as they make a strong kibadachi and I hope everyone faces himself or herself straight and honest. Then when you go back to special training next time, try to find out how you can make an even better kibadachi. Everybody should try that for many years.

We become aware of ourselves through this stance based on reality. Karate is not made up of techniques that somebody invented and then other people just picked up. Karate is the way to find out about our own body, our own minds, our own lives. So everybody try to experience your own hour and a half of kibadachi. We are not standing in kibadachi for any abstract reason. Any idea or practice which is not based on reality is not worth our time.

Fudodachi (Immovable Stance)

Fudodachi means immovable stance. Actually, our minds know how to move easily and our hips are always moving dynamically forward and back and to the side. The reason we call the stance immovable is because we are saying that the opponent can't move us. The stance is exceptionally strong and stable which makes it practical and realistic in combat.

Master Funakoshi's fourth son, Yoshitaka Funakoshi, liked to practice fudodachi and he started the practice of using fudodachi in basics and even in katas. I don't teach fudodachi to the beginners because, from my experience in the early period in California (during the 1950s), if beginners don't learn how to make a solid zenkutsu first, with a strong back leg and strong, supporting hips, they will never be able to make zenkutsu later on. Our early members in California could make fudodachi very well, but they couldn't make zenkutsu.

On the other hand, once you learn how to stand strongly with the back leg and make solid, dynamic hip movements in zenkutsu, it's very easy to learn how to make fudodachi. I'm sure that somebody who can stand in kibadachi for one and a half hours at special training and practices all the time in zenkutsu stance will be able to make fudodachi without difficulty. Just remember that fudodachi has to be really solid. You have to be careful that your back knee doesn't go inward. The back knee has to be like the back knee of kibadachi and bend.

Hangetsu Dachi (Half Moon Stance)

Hangetsu dachi is the stance from the first moves of the kata Hangetsu. When making the Hangetsu stance, your knees are close to protect the centerline, yet they have to be strong against stamping or side thrust kicks. And while the knees push outward, the feet push inward to make the knees very strong in both directions. Never open your centerline to the opponent, no matter what the situation, because the opponent can easily kick your weakest points.

The back foot should point straight toward the opponent, the back heel connects with the punches. When you execute block or attacks, the hips have to be in front of the back heel and the back heel has to be down.

You also must check these points: eyes are watching your opponent's eyes, there is no conscious power in the shoulders, the elbows are in and the underarms are tight. The shoulder blades are in; they are flat against the ribs, not sticking out. With each technique the breathing goes to the fingers or fist or toes.

Shokei and Shorin Stances

Shorin (also known as Shaolin) stances are very extended in one direction such as front stance.

Shokei stances are not like Shorin. They are much narrower but solid and powerful and ready for attacks from all directions. This is the stance that kibadachi and Hangetsu dachi developed from.

When I met the honorary master of the Goju school, Koki Gusukuma (Shiroma), in 1961, he explained his immovable stance. He said the feeling is very heavy — no matter how much you weigh, your feeling goes down through to the earth and nobody can pick you up. At the same time there is a squeezing feeling inside that makes your standing form become very light, so your sensation goes to the air at the same time. Shokei stance is something like that. I hope everybody experiences that feeling.

The Hangetsu stance, the kibadachi stance: these stances are very powerful, but usually this kind of stance works best when the opponent is closer and comes with a swinging motion. The Hangetsu stance is a very narrow stance with both legs and knees strong against the opponent's fumikomi to the knee and hiding all vital points and not showing any centerline.

Blocking and Evading

When you practice blocking, think about why we learn blocks. In a realistic case there are three important points. The first objective is to avoid the attack, which could be deadly. Then, the opponent's momentum must be stopped, breaking his balance and destroying his focus. Finally, you should be ready to destroy the opponent immediately. The counterattack always follows right away.

A block doesn't mean that you put power in your shoulder and arm and then try to hit the opponent's attacking arm. You should not practice blocks with the idea that you are bigger and stronger than all your opponents. That results in sloppy blocks. A block does not mean just avoiding the opponent's attack. You must use your full strength to destroy the opponent's attacking arm or leg. For that your block has to be realistic and effective. An ideal block is one done effectively by a small, light person against a much bigger attacker. There are two requirements to make this ideal block:

First, mentally you've got to feel that you are going to use your maximum energy with the right breathing. Don't lock your breath. Don't take an extra breath before you start. Always execute the block with one feeling, one breathing. And when you touch your opponent's arm or leg, your breathing penetrates the opponent's body. Remember in hand techniques not to stiffen or tense your arm muscles. We use strength momentarily but most of the time there is no conscious power in the shoulders or arms.

Second, we have to learn the basic strength of the body. Your total strength must be in the block. The desired strength comes from many different points. The hips, for example, must be lower than those of your opponent. Your body should be perpendicular to that of the attacker. (This form hides the vital points.) All conscious power is taken out if the shoulders. The elbows should not be sticking out. Keep them within the body line (always remembering that the body line is relative to your opponent). The underarms and hips must be connected to whatever is doing the blocking and connected with the pulling hand. If your arms separate from your body when you block, your power is much less than when you put your elbows in and use the power of your underarms. The key with all blocks is your underarms and the position of your elbow. All this must be supported by a strong stance.

You cannot learn this intellectually. It has to be practiced thousands of times, until you can do it without thinking. For instance, instructors can teach juniors how to make their whole body one unit with the pushing exercise which is used in judo, sumo and other martial arts. Each person tries to get in, pushing with two arms without opening his or her own underarms. If you learn this pushing exercise, with experience you can learn all the important points of blocking an opponent's attack. When you block, only one point on your arm is touching the opponent, but the point is connected to your whole body.

Originally, in karate practice we started with the blocks. At first we did not learn how to punch or kick, we only learned how to block. The instructors felt that we should not harm other people, but only protect ourselves. It was the same when I started to practice. I did not learn how to punch and kick in my first year, I only learned blocks. Seniors could attack with anything, but we would have to use some particular block.

Now I include evading or escaping from attacks without touching hands as blocks but, originally, karate blocks meant not only protecting yourself from an opponent's attack, but also destroying the opponent with strong blocks when they decide to come attack you. In karate, blocks can sometimes be interpreted as attacks.

In America we start with punches and kicks, so it's kind of hard to get the sense of blocks, but every member has to realize that we have to polish our blocks. We must refine our techniques and understanding so that in a real situation we don't make even one mistake.

We start practicing blocks by doing them to the side like the first movement of Heian Shodan. It's much easier for beginners, and even senior members, to block to the side with gedan barai, udeuke, ageuke and shuto-uke. With tetsui we usually step to the front or back.

When blocking to the side, we emphasize a long hanmi (half facing) stance, open hips, strong back leg, no conscious power in the arm or shoulder, the blocking elbow never breaking the body's line and both elbows connected with the underarm on the pulling side. The pulling hand is at the hip, not at the thigh or the ribs. In contrast, the feeling is a little different when we step to the front with tetsui, with the upper body open, swinging and hitting down with rotating hips.

Gedan Barai (Down Block)

Gedan barai is down block, literally lower level sweeping block. We use it against a lower level or middle level attack.

The basic block is made stepping forward in front stance. As you start to step forward, put the blocking fist above the opposite shoulder. Then, with the step, sweep the arm across the body. It stops with the fist about one fist's distance above the blocking side knee just as you finish your step.

We do not make gedan barai just by making the fist hard or by using the power of the arm or the shoulder. This is true for all blocks but it is easiest to learn with gedan barai. Raise both arms, take all of the conscious power out of your arms and shoulders, then drop your arms down to the sides of your body as you make front stance. Everything goes from no power to maximum power, with your mind and breathing and step and hips and arms together.

If you do this warming up exercise before gedan barai, you start to understand what no power to maximum power means, and how the mind always leads the body. Then when you practice gedan barai to the side, you will start to get the feeling of using no power to maximum power to break an opponent's leg when the opponent comes to kick from the side.

Many people hurt their elbow making down block, mainly for two reasons: they either lock their elbow, snapping it every time or their mind is not leading the breathing and the movement. The elbow never locks when you make a down block, and your mind goes first. You are breathing through your arm the whole time, putting your feeling into the arm when you hit the opponent's leg. If you make it that way and don't overextend or lock your elbow, you won't hurt your arm.

Ageuke (Rising Block)

Ageuke means rising block. We use it against an upper level attack.

I find that many people cannot make ageuke. They can do it when I touch and show them, but not by themselves. Even senior members, who can execute it correctly 99 percent of the time, have to consider that in a real fight it might be different, and should always practice executing the correct form of ageuke.

When we make ageuke, it is very easy to see how much trouble your body has following your feeling or your mind. After you get it, after your mind and body become one, it's very easy, very simple. Always, you're ready when your mind is ready. There are three other points to check your technique: power-free, elbows in and small fingers and underarm tight.

First is power-free, which means not relaxed, but taking the conscious power out of your shoulder and arm, even your wrist and fist, but don't open up your fingers. Don't fall asleep, wake up your mind, take the power out from your body and make your mind very strong.

Second, keep your elbow in. If your elbow sticks out, no matter how strong you feel, you cannot connect your mind and body. In all blocks, the position of the elbow is very important.

Third, I emphasize making the small finger and underarm tight. The connection between the small finger and underarm should not be overlooked.

The best way to practice this block, especially in the beginning, is by moving to the side. This training method is most useful for blocks where we use the side of our body. It is much easier to execute all blocks — ageuke, udeuke and shuto-uke or even gedan barai — to the side because you can easily connect the blocking arm with the rest of the parts of your body, back leg, hips, both underarms and pulling hand, and because you don't twist your hips.

Your strongest form when you block is with both hips on one line toward the opponent. When you make ageuke, block with your whole body connected. The elbow never sticks out from the body's line, power never goes up to the shoulder and arm, the blocking elbow connects to the underarm, the underarm connects to the hip and the hips connect to your stance. Then you can block.

To practice this, begin standing facing to the front in natural stance. Step directly to the left and make front stance with the left leg forward, turning the right foot toward the left, too. Do not change the angle of the hips or shoulders. In other words, the upper body does not face to the left. It is still exactly sideways. Then just raise your arm in ageuke without conscious power in the shoulder. Keep your elbow on the line and the small finger tight and connected with the underarm. This underarm is not strongly tight. I usually use the words "slightly tight" but there should be almost no conscious tightening.

The movement of the arm as you raise it is a half-circle beginning at the solar plexus and moving up toward the chin and then forward away from the head. The arm should not make a half circle moving forward and then back. It should move closer and then out toward the opponent. The actual block is with the forearm, not the fist or elbow. When the block is completed, the back of the forearm is just in front of the forehead. There is a straight line from the blocking elbow through the front shoulder to the back shoulder. Any angle in the shoulder makes this block much weaker.

The small finger connects with the underarm and then the hips, and this line connects to the back heel. This way, anybody can make ageuke without trouble, even a small person against a large, powerful opponent. One more small point, the forearm of the blocking arm doesn't go back. From the elbow it is held up ninety degrees from the blocking direction (the line directly towards your opponent), with the blocking elbow on the body line. First, practice this ideal form, then from natural stance you can block in any direction with ageuke. Of course, you should make our traditional practice of making ageuke stepping with front stance and back stance, too.

Udeuke (Forearm Block)

Udeuke means forearm block. We use it against middle level and upper level attacks.

We make this block stepping forward in front stance or to the side from natural stance. As you start to step, move your arm across your body so that the blocking hand is in front of the opposite shoulder with the fingers facing back. Bring the arm across your body with the arm rotating so that the fingers always point backwards until it stops in front of the blocking shoulder. The elbow is about one fist from the body. Fist, elbow, both shoulders and both hips are all on one line toward the opponent. The wrist is bent to make a slight hook to catch the opponent's arm.

Udeuke is actually a quite revolutionary block. When we think about the natural way to block, maybe the way gorillas block, we swat at the attack like tetsui. The arm goes from the outside to the inside. But this block goes from the inside to the outside. It is a very different feeling and our mentality must be completely different. Instead of pushing the attack and the opponent farther away, we can now penetrate into the opponent with our block, especially when we make blocks like movements 11 and 13 in Bassai. Then the opponent has very few ways to continue his attack and we can make a powerful counterattack with enpi or fumikomi right away.

Because udeuke is not a natural movement like tetsui or uraken, it can be very difficult for beginners. But think of it later on, once you know how to make realistic blocks. Using a very small motion of the wrist and with the correct elbow position, you can block most chudan or jodan attacks very realistically with this udeuke motion.

Of course, we have to learn a big, dynamic motion first, because in the beginning nobody can make a small motion effectively or realistically. After that we work on powerful motions and then quick motions, in that order. Later on, these motions become very small, very quick, without conscious power, yet are still very effective.

To make powerful and realistic blocks, especially udeuke, you have to use the whole body, with the correct shoulder and elbow position. One way to practice the correct position of the shoulder and elbow is to hook arms with each other in kibadachi and then punch and block each other.

Both people make kibadachi at about a 45° angle to each other and make udeuke (with the same arm) so that the wrists are just touching. Slowly at first, you punch toward your partner. Your partner keeps the punch from hitting with the udeuke. Then your partner makes a punch toward you and you block it with udeuke. Keep your wrists touching at all times. Go back and forth speeding up until you are doing the practice quite fast, but still with good form.

After this practice, I'm sure many people have very tired shoulders and arms. Later you will start to understand how to make this practice without using conscious power in your shoulder and arm muscles, using only your underarms and always being conscious of the position of your elbows. This is a very good practice to develop underarm muscles, especially for people with weak arms or less underarm muscles. For example, ladies with smaller arms can be very powerful with a strong underarm muscle.

Tetsui (Hammer Block)

Tetsui comes from "te" which means hand and "tsui" which means hammer so tetsui means hand hammer. Some people spell tetsui as "tettsui" using "tetsu" which means iron instead of "te" but this is really just slang. They are saying that the fist should be as hard as iron. Other people call the technique uchikomi which means the dynamic action of getting in and hitting the opponent with an iron hammer.

Tetsui can be both block and attack. When this technique is executed, the arm should swing up to a high position. It should be slightly outside of the body line so that the arm opens up just a bit. The elbow should not be bent very much but be careful not to lock the arm. The arm should not swing behind the body line. The hand then swings down to a position in front of the opposite shoulder. When you swing the fist up, only use power in the small fingers. Take conscious power completely out of the fist and wrist, arms and shoulder, until the moment you hit the opponent. Then your power explodes and this fist connects with every other part of the body.

Tetsui is an old, primitive technique and most human beings can learn how to execute it very powerfully. It is one of the natural movements. Even apes know this motion. Without any training, people can use this technique.

Historically, karate people have not practiced tetsui as much as the other blocks, but you should practice this technique. If you don't have effective techniques in your practice, you should work on natural techniques like this. After only several thousand times, it can be very realistic.

Shuto-uke (Sword Hand Block)

Shuto-uke means sword hand block. Most of the time we say "knife hand," but "sword hand" is a more exact translation.

This block is actually a combination of two different techniques. First there is a sweeping block to knock an opponent's attack away. Second, we are going into the opponent.

To make the sword hand first hold your forearm straight out in front of you, relaxed, with the wrist joint straight. The hand and forearm make a straight line. Second, without bending the wrist at all, arch the hand and fingers backwards. Do not bend your wrist. Third, keeping the wrist straight and the hand arched, curl the ends of the fingers inward slightly as if to start grasping the handle of a tool. Do not bend the palm of the hand. Do not bend the finger inward toward the palm at the palm-knuckle joint. Remember to curl the fingers slightly. The thumb has to be correct, neither opened up or bent excessively towards the little finger. Practice this sequence one step at a time, faster and faster until you can do it in one motion and one feeling.

When Master Funakoshi taught shuto-uke, he always demonstrated that the hand came from the opposite ear. So begin with the blocking hand open and the inside of the palm covering your opposite ear. When you make this block, the front and rear elbows cross and the underarms connect. Every time you block, your breathing goes to the small finger edge of the hand, the blade of the sword, which extends from your little finger to your elbow. Your elbow never breaks the body's line and elbows move with your lats and hips. Your stance must also be strong so make back stance with your hips in front of your back heel. Otherwise, if the opponent comes to push, you will fall down. Your back heel never comes up and your toes never turn to the back. Bend the ankle and knee, keep your hips low and your front leg free to make a strong kick.

Also, many people let the rear shoulder go up. Keep both shoulders down and horizontal, emphasize tight underarms and take the conscious power out of both the shoulders and arms. Block with your whole mind and make your breathing come to your fingertips every time you block.

When a technique is performed with open hands, as with shuto-uke and spear hand, the fingers can be hurt more easily than when they are in a fist. To strengthen the fingers we need to put our mind at the fingertips. This is done through breathing. You can try this breathing by pushing an opponent with your index finger. If you make your breath and feeling go through the finger as you push, you will be able to move your opponent. On the other hand, if you are thinking about something else or your breathing and feeling are not strong enough, your finger will not be strong enough to push your opponent.

This is not an easy block. Master Funakoshi practiced this technique each morning and he did not understand it until he was quite old. You have to repeat this block many times before it will be realistic against bigger opponents.

Morote-Uke (Two Hand Block)

Morote-uke comes from "moro" which means both, "te" which means hands and "uke" which means block, so morote-uke means blocks with both hands or arms.

Especially for people who are short or light and have small arms, when facing a powerful opponent with huge arms, one arm is often not strong enough. However, if you block with both arms together and any part of the hands touching, the block is 100% stronger. People, especially those with smaller bodies, have to learn how to block with both arms. Examples include the double rising block (movement 22) in Bassai and the middle level double hand blocks (movements 22, 23 and 24) in Heian Yodan. Other morote-uke where the hands don't touch include the opening moves in Heian Nidan and Heian Yodan.

Blocks with both arms are very powerful, effective and realistic because we move the whole body together. When both arms move together with your hips, upper body and strong standing leg, the block is always effective. Keep both shoulders down, underarms tight, chest and back open and block without shrinking, with a strong stance. Practice this and apply it in kumite.

Kakiwake (Opening Technique)

Kakiwake is like movement 14 in Heian Yodan. After we execute uraken and turn to the rear into back stance, the open hands make a fist, with the fists stopping in front of both shoulders, spreading the opponent's grab apart. The back of the fists should be facing up, or the hands may be open with the palms facing up or down. Elbows should be inside the body's line. Pull back with the hips, not just the arms. This is one of the escaping techniques you can apply in a real situation when an opponent starts to grab your collar.

Kakiwake without an opponent is very different than kakiwake with an opponent, so it is a good idea to practice this movement with a friend. When the opponent starts to grab your collar, try to escape from the opponent's grasp, keeping the elbows in and connecting your underarms. Keep your hips low and don't let them get behind your back foot or your opponent can easily knock you down.

When we practice kakiwake, we always move with our hips and power in the underarms. It is very easy to say this but hard to realize and experience. Until you experience an opponent grabbing your body or collar with both hands, you never realize that the only chance to get out is to keep the elbows inside the body's line. Only if you do the movement properly, can you force an opening for your own front kick by bringing the opponent's arms out.

When you practice with your friend, communicate with him. For instance, if you try to use shoulder power, he can tell you that you are doing the motion incorrectly. If you relax your shoulders, keep your elbows in, connect them with your underarms and lower your hips, the technique will be effective and your friend can tell you that it works. You must exchange this kind of information with your friend.

Instructors have to teach kakiwake in this realistic situation because most beginners don't know why they have to hold the elbows inside the line of the body. If the elbows go outside of the body's line just a little bit, this block doesn't work.

If the opponent is big and you are small or if the opponent's hold is very strong, even a block with good form may not work. In that case put your hands together and use both your arms together in a morote-uke inside and take away the opponent's grab one hand at a time. Then you can escape. But if you are the same size or bigger as long as you use your hips, you can make the opening hands effective.

The best timing for your block and escape is the moment the opponent starts to grab you, not after the opponent is holding your shirt or your body very tightly. At that moment, open up your opponent's arms with your arms. Once an opponent is holding you, especially if you are lighter against a bigger opponent, it is much more difficult to escape.

Of course the block by itself is not enough. Just as you finish the block, unbalance your opponent by pulling your opponent's upper body towards you, and in their weak moment, kick to an exact vital point.

Yamagamae (Mountain Posture)

Yamagamae means mountain posture. It comes from the Japanese character for mountain (山) which looks like someone with their arms above their head.

This form doesn't work if your elbow is even a little bit lower or higher than the shoulder. Your elbows have to be exactly shoulder level, and also exactly to the sides. And be careful not to use any conscious power in your shoulder, keep your underarms slightly tight and never lock your shoulder blades together in the middle of the back. Without the correct form, this block will never be effective. Therefore, you must practice with a friend and test this block so that you can find out how to make it effective and realistic, and understand that when your arms come up without power you can still block against an opponent's strong attack.

Sabaki (Evading)

The word sabaki means evading. In sabaki, we are not trying to escape from the opponent. Our mentality, our eye contact, goes into the opponent, while the body evades. This is different from what we feel when we are weak and want to get out of danger and our hips cannot move correctly. For sabaki you must keep a strong feeling.

We use sabaki in many places. One very important one is sanbon gumite when we defend without blocks. Another is when we are practicing against kicks. The opponent comes to kick very quickly but, while they're kicking, they are standing on only one leg. The evading side using two legs should be able to get out if he stays cool.

I think instructors should teach evading with hips' motions to beginners or junior members, because even in the worst case when you cannot move, if you twist your hips, you can avoid most of an opponent's attacks.

Effective Blocks

Ideally, any block can be an attack, so we must always make powerful blocks. If you just lightly touch your opponent's kicking leg or punching arm without making a focus or unbalancing your opponent, you cannot stop an opponent's aggressive attack. If you cannot touch your opponent's arms or legs with an effective focus when you block, it's better not to touch at all.

If all you are doing is touching your opponent to confirm where their hands or legs are, so that you can feel comfortable in your mind for one moment, this is silly. You have to cut off that kind of emotion. When you block, you have to destroy or at least unbalance your opponent and make your counterattack during the moment they are unbalanced. Here there are two different timings: one where you block and counterattack simultaneously, another where you unbalance your opponent and then counterattack.

Blocks Against Kicks

We must be able to handle an opponent's realistic and powerful kicks. We use gedan barai and sweeping blocks, both from the inside and the outside, to take advantage of the opponent when he kicks.

When we make gedan barai, actually we are crushing the opponent's toes, ankles or shin as part of the counterattack. When we make gedan barai in a real situation, we must execute it very strongly. Many people are missing this part these days.

Of course, in practice we have to be careful and not hurt each other. Practice does not mean showing the opponent, "I'm superior to you." Practice means both asking each other humbly to continue practicing together for many years with a strong, realistic feeling — with each taking responsibility for protecting the other's body from injury.

Also, blocking with open hands is dangerous because there is a chance of damage to your fingers. If you damage your fingers, this is often permanent damage. Therefore, in the beginning always keep your small fingers tight, make a fist and avoid accidents when you practice blocks against kicks.

Blocking with the arms is not the only way to handle kicks. It used to be that when somebody tried to kick middle level, we would not always step back. Instead, we would step *in* before the opponent's kick was strong, and just push back with our stomach. Taking the opponent's kick like that will make you lose in a tournament. That's why some realistic movements like these disappear, but we should keep them anyway as part of our realistic practice.

Fist

If you really hit with your whole strength, unless you make the correct fist and wrist, you can damage your fingers, knuckles and your wrist. Therefore, everybody has to find the strongest way to make a fist.

First, open your hand, extending the fingers completely and look at the base of your thumb for a little hole (slight indentation). This hole indicates that your wrist and hand and forearm are completely connected. Then, you tighten your small finger, then your third, second and index fingers. You can extend the index finger from the first knuckle or bend it under. Finally, tighten your thumb inward across the index finger. This is the strongest form for the fist.

Depending on your level, there is some difference in how much power you should use to hold your fist. In the beginning, you should always make a tight fist strongly because it's easy to forget about your hand and let your fingers get loose enough to be hurt. To get used to making a fist hit your makiwara or your hanging bag. When I was young, I was hitting a minimum of 200 times every day for the first three years, so I recommend that junior members hit a soft target lightly every day. It is not necessary to hit a very hard board or hard object — that is not only not necessary, it is very bad and can damage the bones in your hand or wrist. Be sure you hit a bag or makiwara that is not too hard, hit carefully, lightly and regularly.

After you have the habit of making a really good, solid fist, you can practice making only the small finger tight with almost no power while still keeping the proper form of the fist.

Oizuki (Front Punch)

"Oi" means chase after or follow and "tsuki" ("zuki") means thrust. We also call this technique front punch.

We have a saying, "Start with oizuki and end with oizuki." The whole understanding of oizuki is to always go back to oizuki and strive to make it the strongest and most perfect one.

Oizuki is one of the most difficult basics because human beings naturally want to face the opponent and stand solid, not moving much, maybe sliding to the side or back. Stepping in requires a courageous mind in front of a strong opponent. If you can move your hips dynamically toward the opponent without losing your balance and without making a weaker stance, it is very powerful because all of your weight, focus and momentum goes into the opponent and into the effectiveness of the punch.

Our seniors and geniuses found that oizuki is one of the exceptional techniques, so in Shotokan we practice it from the beginning. Even though we know that it is a difficult mission, we all practice oizuki with the hips as low as possible. Some critics, practitioners and especially modern tournament players think this is ridiculous because, if you keep your hips low, you cannot move quickly and the opponent can take the advantage. They don't want to make lower hips and they sometimes laugh at our practice because they think we have unrealistic movements, but there are some deep considerations here. To become strong you have to have a courageous mind. In the beginning, we are all cowards. We are lazy and weak, but we can become strong, courageous and powerful if we change our mentality. So as a training method, we practice moving our lazy, cowardly hips dynamically to the front, with strong willpower, every day. This is the most important element of oizuki practice.

These are the other important points when making a basic oizuki. The front hip goes first, straight forward. The front knee bends so the hips can go straight forward without any movement upward. The body all goes forward at once. There should be no conscious power in the shoulder or arm, just a little tension (or strength) in the underarm of the pulling hand. To make a punch, eyes go first, then hips, then hand. This means that the strength of the punch comes from concentrating all of the power of the body and mind.

You can check the points of your oizuki form with this list. First, make a correct fist; second, maintain a strong back leg; third, keep the toes of your back foot in; fourth, keep underarms and lats strong, on the pulling side as well as on the attacking side; fifth, breathe through your wrist and fist; sixth, thrust your hips through the imaginary opponent's body. Seventh, in the ending form for oizuki, the fist and shoulder, hips and front and back leg are all on the line. Your mind goes to the line with the hips, exactly. Execute each of these points with a strong mind.

If you look at the ideal form of the thrust, maete and the last part of oizuki are the same. The ideal technique has energy going through the opponent with oneness, with the back heel, front hip, underarm and fist all connected. When you extend with a strong penetrating mind, the shoulder cannot be stuck. It has to follow the fist. When making maete and oizuki, the shoulder goes in to the opponent, too.

Never be satisfied with your oizuki until you execute it with oneness of your mind and body, top and bottom, inside and outside, including timing and breathing. With one feeling you can reach the opponent without any minor movements. Everything has to be one, with your mind penetrating the opponent before you execute your thrusting attack. We should all try to reach a level, mentally, physically and technically, where we can execute oizuki to a bigger, tougher, stronger opponent. This is extremely difficult.

I practiced oizuki stepping to the front all the time and it took me many years to understand. Oizuki is a difficult form for beginners to make correctly stepping forward. However, I think that if you practice oizuki to the side with oneness, mentally and physically, with the correct breathing and dynamic hip movements, you can understand and improve much more quickly, eliminating up to 50 percent of the practice time.

Practicing oizuki (or maete) to the side, is like gedan barai to the side. You can practice the form by extending a finger pointing to the side and then making a fist. Beginners can make the ideal form of oizuki very easily, with low hips and a strong back leg. Make your hips go in and your mind go through your fist, very quickly and with one feeling. Don't forget that you have to apply this same feeling to oizuki from a front stance. Make a gedan barai to the front, then step and attack. Do it the same way whether to the side or to the front.

Even if you can learn oizuki faster by practicing it to the side, you still must do oizuki many times. Numbers are important. We have to make oizuki without discussion until we can make the ideal form without conscious thought. Every day, every time we practice, we try to find the mental maturity to be patient, to be strong for a long time, to push ourselves hard and continuously. Our conscious, intellectual understanding is not enough.

Maybe because I am trying to interest members in this simple practice, I explain too much, but discussion or explanation will never bring you a good oizuki. We have to practice until our unconscious, our body, understands. In other words, your feeling, your execution, with the hips and with the strong stance and pulling hand, all these elements you always see and criticize and think about before and after practice. During oizuki practice, concentrate on making your best execution, with your strongest feeling with each punch. To make ideal, effective, realistic oizuki takes a million times.

We make 1,000 oizuki at midnight practice in special training, and seniors can increase that number for their own practice, but they shouldn't lead extreme numbers for juniors. Especially don't get the idea that you want to shock juniors by suddenly leading oizuki from the beginning to the end of a practice. You will only discourage them with this kind of showing off. Senior members can practice more, but for juniors, 200 times is enough, 500 times at the most, but not more than that.

Leaders have to realize that not all members are at the same level and remember that when we started, we were all lazy, cowardly and weak. After years of training, people start to forget how they were as beginners. When we are young, we want to be proud of ourselves, come up to a good level and show off. We have to resist such a temptation. To lead is not to show off. You have to consider the level of your students and what is important for them. You have to be patient to bring them up little by little.

I know some instructors like to make a 1,000-oizuki practice. Could you have made 1,000 oizuki in the first week, first month or even the first year when you started? If somebody did that to you, you would have quit the very next day, but you want to do it to your juniors. To lead juniors, you have to make a practice that is just a little bit difficult for them and encourage them to increase their ability. One day they will be ready to make 1,000 oizuki.

After you start to understand oizuki, I don't think you will have a problem with maete. Maete is just a short oizuki, the last part of the oizuki or oizuki is a dynamic movement of maete. Also think about what parts of oizuki are different from gyakuzuki, the realistic viewpoints, effectiveness, efficiency, and then form and speed and how to get oneness.

Gyakuzuki (Reverse Punch)

Gyakuzuki means reverse punch. "Gyaku" means reverse and "tsuki" ("zuki") means thrust.

We make the basic form for gyakuzuki by making zenkutsu and extending open hands to the side. Both the hips and the arms are perpendicular to the direction we are facing. The fingers and the thumb are together with the thumb on top. Next move your arms to the front without lowering your hands or bending your arms. Your body stays squarely facing the opponent and your hands meet together in front. Leave the punching hand in place and make a pulling hand on the hip with the opposite hand. If you push on the punching hand, this energy goes back to the back heel. Stand with the back leg supporting your hips and body. Your front leg is bent but most of your weight is on the back leg.

Once you find the exact position of the fist and both shoulders and the position of the hips and back heel at the end of the gyakuzuki, you have to remember it so you can finish there each time you punch. As much as you can, push in to the front. Even the forehead should not lean back, but goes forward with the hips. These are the points to check for gyakuzuki:

1. The back toe has to be in.
2. The back leg is straight but the back knee never really locks.
3. The front knee doesn't go back. It has to be free so it can go in toward the opponent.
4. Don't rotate your hips. They go straight in.
5. Your spine and head go with your hips.
6. Both shoulders are down. They both face front, straight and square. The shoulders are never pulled back, so that they pinch the shoulder blades together in the middle of the back, making what I call a "chicken wing."
7. Both shoulders go in together.
8. Underarms connect the punch to the hips.
9. The pulling hand is in the proper position.
10. Everything must be kept on line from the punch to the back heel.
11. Breathing goes with the punch.

Everything must go in through your opponent with one motion, all together, with the power going through your two knuckles. Move your hips dynamically and then go into the opponent simultaneously with punch and hips and pulling hand. Your strong mentality can make these go together.

I have emphasized for many years that the final, ideal form is an important part of the strength of the technique. However, even if you know the final form of gyakuzuki, if you don't execute it many times, it will not work. You should emphasize not only the correct final form, but also increase the number of techniques. When you make gyakuzuki in practice, make it at least 200 times. (Actually you can never make gyakuzuki enough.) Always try to find where you are wasting power and energy. Then you can find a realistic, strong reverse punch.

Gyakuzuki with Rotating Hips:

In addition to a thrusting gyakuzuki, we also practice a swinging gyakuzuki where both the hips and the hand make a swinging motion. When making gyakuzuki with rotating hips, make strong, powerful hip movements and make a swinging punch. This time there is no conscious power in the shoulders or in the arm. Only make the small finger tight, swinging with the hips. This fist connects through the underarm and then penetrates the opponent. This is not basic gyakuzuki and you must understand that this technique doesn't work when the hips and arms make different motions. If the hips are turning and the fist is thrusting, the technique will not be effective.

Applications of Gyakuzuki:

We practice three ways for applying a basic gyakuzuki:
1. Lift the front knee to the front arm's elbow. Jump in and attack.
2. Remain in the original position, attack at the same time as your opponent attacks, but finish before he does.
3. Step back as the opponent attacks, get away and make a block with the front hand or arm and counterattack with gyakuzuki.

To be effective in this practice, you must concentrate on timing and distance.

Gyakuzuki Practice:

One way to practice gyakuzuki is to emphasize the back heel, the back leg and their connection to the fist. When you make the punch in zenkutsu, the back leg and back heel have to connect to the fist.

Another way to practice is to make the punch to the side from kibadachi stance. With this solid stance we can make an effective attack. This is like kokutsu in the beginning of Heian Godan, where we make gyakuzuki after udeuke, with the emphasis on the back leg, especially the back heel staying on the ground and connecting with the execution of the gyakuzuki.

When making gyakuzuki with kibadachi-zuki to the side, little by little, turn open the front knee and toes, then it's easier to make the hips go into the opponent. This also makes it easier to make hips and hands go together. The shoulders must stay down, elbows in, underarms tight. Don't turn your hips all the way. They go straight in. The back knee stays out.

Sometimes you should practice basic ippon gumite and sanbon gumite using only gyakuzuki as your counterattack. No matter how you move to avoid the attack, you have to make a solid stance with strong hips when you execute the reverse punch. The back heel and the back leg must be connected with your hip movements and with the execution of the arms.

Another way to practice gyakuzuki is to take the conscious power out of the upper arm and to almost completely relax, except for the small finger which should be tightened to make a fist. When you execute gyakuzuki, as soon as you touch the opponent's body, your whole power penetrates with your subconscious mind and breathing, extending through your hips, arm, wrist and fist. If you practice this way, your gyakuzuki will become very effective and much quicker. Many people are tensing the muscles in the upper arm and forearm. This makes the punch slower because the power in the muscles acts like the brakes on a car, slowing then stopping your movements. The key is to find out how to take off the power when you start the punch and finish the technique with one motion of the fist and hips.

Consider making a realistic gyakuzuki. We should be able to apply gyakuzuki when our opponent is moving, and we need to have the ability to execute this technique moving in or out. To do this, a good sense of timing and distance is necessary. Try to apply this technique in jiyu kumite practice.

Oizuki and Gyakuzuki (Front Punch and Reverse Punch)

Looking at the difference between oizuki and gyakuzuki is important for two reasons. The first is to understand the difference between the techniques. The second is to remind ourselves that each of us has the opportunity to practice seriously and discover something new in karate.

For many years, karate teachers did not teach the real differences between oizuki and gyakuzuki. Many people misunderstood and just punched. In the 1940s, 1950s and 1960s especially, many Shotokan groups were mixed up and were teaching the wrong method to juniors.

Now, theoretically, it's very clear what the differences between oizuki and gyakuzuki are. In the ending form for oizuki, the fist and shoulder, hips and front and back leg are all on one line. Your mind goes exactly along the line of the hips toward the opponent. This is the same feeling as kibadachi-zuki, with the fist and all other parts of the body on one line. In other words, oizuki is a one-line punch.

On the other hand, gyakuzuki is made with your whole body facing straight (with the width of the body at a ninety degree angle to the line of the punch).

Why is there this difference? One reason is that your back foot has to connect with the punch and the other is that the shoulders have to connect to the rest of the body. These are two hints, but to understand the difference can be really difficult.

I've explained these ideas for many years, but everybody should have the attitude and habit to think about the question: what are the real differences between oizuki and gyakuzuki? These days you cannot attack somebody's body to test your ideas, but there are ways to find how your movements and body position change the effectiveness of a technique. So, everybody should try to think as an original karate practitioner. Study the difference between oizuki and gyakuzuki as a way to learn how to research questions about karate practice.

One important point is that you must practice enough so that you can execute either one, depending on the situation, without conscious thought. For me, oizuki and gyakuzuki are like a two-strand rope. Maybe you would say that they are two sides of the same coin. As you attack an opponent, you must be able to use one or the other as the situation requires. At one distance the best technique is gyakuzuki but at another distance it is oizuki. You don't even have to think which is which because your body just knows how to connect effectively at each distance. This is like the spiral of the rope. One moment it is oizuki and then the next twist is gyakuzuki and the next twist is oizuki, actually depending on the distance between you and your opponent. Your hip movement and steps are different, but there is one continuous movement of your mind.

Basic oizuki and gyakuzuki are thrusting techniques, so don't get either mixed up with swinging techniques or swinging hips. We have swinging techniques with rotating hips, but when you practice penetrating techniques on the line, the mentality and feeling always have to penetrate to the opponent's vital points. In this way oizuki and gyakuzuki are the same.

Maete (Jab)

Maete means front hand. Maete is usually a jab like the last part of the oizuki but maete can be any attack with the front hand.

As you can see in boxing matches, maete is one of the most realistic hand techniques. It has the same basic importance in our practice because there is no difference between realistic, effective techniques in karate and boxing. Every boxer learns the jab first and practices it over and over. We should do the same in karate.

While you are making maete many times, you have to find out when it is effective, which way is quickest, how you can hit the opponent and where. Maete is a very short motion so the power of the arm is not enough. In one short attack maete has to connect with your whole body and be part of your physical movement.

Be aware of the following points when you make maete. Your hand, arm and shoulder must be almost completely relaxed, with no conscious power. With one feeling you penetrate the opponent's vital point, first with your mentality and then with your fist which is connected to your underarms, hips, back leg and back foot. Make everything become one at the last second. That is the key to making a maete with kime (focused power).

The angles of the fist, arm and shoulder, upper chest and stance are also important. Try to find the correct angle to make the most realistic, effective maete. When you extend your punch with a strong, penetrating mind, the shoulder isn't stuck. It has to follow the fist. Therefore, when making maete, the shoulder goes toward the opponent.

When we practice orthodox katas and basics, sometimes we start to be unrealistic in real combat. So I expect everyone to practice this technique which is very realistic and effective close to the opponent.

Seniors practicing maete can use this practice to become sensitive to the moment in which the opponent decides to come to destroy you and learn to get into the opponent at that moment. This is the practice of "sen-no-sen". In this practice the maete is not a mechanical hand technique. You are studying how to read your opponent's mind. All of us should have confidence in the human mental ability to sense the moment an opponent is starting to attack.

The third movement in Heian Nidan is actually maete with back stance. In the kata we make maete in back stance, but this is a very difficult technique. When you start to learn maete, I think it's better to stand in front stance.

Maete Applications:
Consider the following points when you study how to apply maete.
1. Don't show your attack.
2. Don't expose yourself to your opponent's attack.
3. Be careful of ma (distance and timing).
4. Practice for speed by relaxing the arm and shoulder.
5. Research combinations of techniques besides a jab to use with the front hand (maete).
    a. maete as attack with ippon ken (one knuckle attack) or nukite (spear hand)
    b. maete as gyakuzuki with the other leg stepping in
    c. maete as uraken
    d. maete as uraken stepping in with the opposite leg
6. The importance of maete lies in timing. Sen-no-sen means your best moment to attack is when your opponent decides to attack.
7. If timing, focus or distance is wrong, you can't make the technique work.

Maete to the Side:
We should practice maete to the side, too. I have found that people can move their hips to the side much easier than stepping forward. I want to see all beginners connect the mind and the fist and the hips together. The mind goes first, the breathing follows your mind, then the body goes. In maete, body, fist and hips simultaneously move together with the pulling hand. This form is like the final form of oizuki, which everybody knows.

From shizentai (natural stance), step directly to the left or right with opening hips and make maete. The important point in this practice is that the mind has to lead the body. Without first feeling or imagining an opponent to the side, your movements cannot be strong or quick or powerful. The mind goes first and the body follows. Learn to imagine opponents to the side and always penetrate realistically with one motion. Some members have a habit of inhaling when they start to move. They must learn to avoid this bad habit, especially in this maete practice to the side.

Because maete has to be on the line of the body, it is very useful to first teach moving to the side with a thrusting attack. After several hundred times practicing to the side, you can practice another technique with maete (perhaps uraken). I think that helps us understand how to coordinate the body with the mind, and how maete connects with hip movements.

Kibadachi-zuki (Punch from Horse Riding Stance)

Kibadachi-zuki is a punch like oizuki or maete made from kibadachi. These days, with the emphasis on tournament-style practice, few people realize how effective kibadachi-zuki is. Shotokan members should be able to find this stance and this most effective attack with refined kime (focus of power). Someday in a real, critical situation, it will help you.

When you start to practice kibadachi-zuki, punch just to the side with no step because kibadachi is much easier and stronger to the side. Remember to always thrust with the hip. To make the hip go with the thrusting fist, we must make the heels go out. Therefore, attack with the hips and keep the heels out. And when you thrust, your attacking fist and front and back shoulders are all on the line and the back shoulder never goes up. Tighten your rear underarm and connect it with the attacking fist, then connect fist and underarm with the stance. That's how you make the most effective thrust.

Another way to practice kibadachi-zuki is stepping in or stepping back from natural stance. For instance, pivot on the left leg and step back with the right leg, attacking with the left hand. Or, step in with the right leg and attack with the right hand. You should also practice these techniques in basic ippon gumite. When the opponent comes with a right hand attack, step back with the right leg, blocking the opponent's right hand attack with your right hand, your left hand counterattacking to your opponent's right armpit. You have to control your counterattack exactly so you don't even touch because you can damage your opponent's ribs easily.

After many repetitions to the side, begin thrusting to the front and back. Remember to cover your weak points with the rear hand. People feel very uncomfortable stepping this way, but if you keep your stepping foot straight along the line to your opponent (feet come together and then the foot steps out), it makes it much easier to move quickly to the opponent. This tsuki, or thrust technique, is very effective if you make a solid kibadachi and connect with the underarms. This is one of the easiest ways to make kime.

We also practice this as a counterattack in jiyu-ippon gumite, which is the most realistic kumite practice. Even then you should be able to execute your counterattack with the strongest kibadachi-zuki. Junior members, especially those who don't have big bodies and arms, should practice this technique. This is a good way to learn how to make a realistic and effective technique with your strongest focus.

A third way to make kibadachi-zuki is to slide in and attack. After you get used to it, make your movements free and execute your technique. Always be conscious of the rear standing leg.

[For more information about punching from kibadachi, see the discussion of kibadachi in the section on stances.]

Suwari-zuki (Sitting Attack)

"Suwari" means sitting and "tsuki" ("zuki") means thrust so this is making a punch starting in the sitting position. Why do we make this clumsy practice? Because everybody has weaknesses in their hip movements, not only in practice but in their real combat stance. Sitting form is the traditional martial arts practice to improve hip movements.

The hips are the center of the body and, when they move freely, the body moves freely. Strength comes from the hip movement. This practice enables your hips to go with your strong mind. No matter how strong your mind is, without practice the hips don't move. Especially in real situations, the hips are heavy and lazy. If you can begin to move your hips from sitting form, when you stand, your hips will be much lighter and move much more easily.

In modern society, most human beings don't know how to use their hips properly because they don't use them very often. We don't walk very far, we don't bump into each other frequently and we are always sitting in a comfortable seat or in a car, so we are losing the mobility of our hips.

There's no real occasion these days where somebody would come attack you when you're sitting like this, so this is not a practice for a real situation. However, there is no other way to practice the refined hip movements we find in sitting form. We have to use our hips more strongly, more powerfully, with a strong mentality because we can't use our legs in this practice. Therefore even though sitting forms are uncomfortable, awkward and painful for modern people, we maintain this kind of old-fashioned, oriental custom of making sitting movements.

The best sitting practice is oizuki. Do this practice in front of a wall or makiwara. Just sit like in mokuso, then make the fist and hips go together, thrusting into the opponent. You have to have a courageous, strong mind first, then your hips will be lighter.

In the early 1960s, I made many of the senior members practice this to acquire strong hips. We sacrificed the skin on our knees, shins and feet, but the practice was very valuable for our hips. We still need to make this practice, but now I think it is acceptable to wear some type of knee pad if you're going to practice this for a long period of time.

The only people who should avoid this practice are those with knee or ankle problems. Sitting form will make the problem worse, so make the practice with standing form as long as the problem lasts.

I hope everybody practices sitting form because it makes your hip movements much more dynamic and flexible. Making movements from this position helps develop smooth, quick and free hip motions.

Uraken (Back Fist)

Uraken means back fist. "Ura" is back and "ken" is fist.

Uraken is one of the most powerful techniques and without much training you can execute it very effectively. I think originally, maybe a few million years ago, all apes used this movement as a powerful attack. This is a very primitive movement. I don't mean primitive in a bad way, but that it is one of the original, natural, human movements. You see it in Heian Nidan, Heian Yodan and Empi.

This was my first favorite technique. I remember in 1948 getting a back punch on the nose that destroyed me completely and I was very impressed, so I practiced it a lot. One year I hit back punch every day at least 200 times with each fist. That made me different, I think, punching on the makiwara every day for a year. I was so proud when, during this time, at special training one senior said, "Oh, everybody stop. Look at this guy. I'm sure this guy is practicing back punch every day." I was so happy. So maybe that's the reason uraken feels very natural to me, especially when I saw an orangutan in a zoo make a really good back punch and a gorilla made a good one, too. I felt, they are my brothers.

No matter how modernized and sophisticated human beings become, we should not forget these original techniques. This is especially true for the short, light person who doesn't have much power in hand techniques. He can still make realistic and effective backfist attacks. We should all practice uraken until we are confident that, even against bigger, experienced opponents, we can make realistic kime (focused power) in our counterattacks.

You can learn this technique in a short period of time. If you do this technique maybe 10,000 or 20,000 times, you can already use it effectively. In other words, compared with oizuki or gyakuzuki, where it can take a million times to find some realistic sense and effectiveness, with just 10,000 uraken you can reach a good level. If you do it 100,000 times, it becomes very effective. For one tenth of the effort, you get a much larger result compared with oizuki. If you don't have definite, effective techniques in your practice, you should stick with natural techniques like this one. Everybody should pick some form of uraken as one of your favorite techniques.

We practice three different methods of making uraken. This is because uraken can go any direction, not just to the side.

The first one is from kibadachi. Swing to the side tightening both underarms simultaneously. Make a pulling hand when you execute the uraken.

The second practice is exactly as in Tekki Shodan, hitting down. After blocking to the side, execute uraken to the front. Your fist should stop in front of your mouth. You are attacking your opponent's nose, the chin or even the chest, while standing in a narrow kibadachi. You can also make this hitting down feeling stepping forward like the uraken in movement 13 of Heian Yodan or with kibadachi to the side like movement 13 of Heian Sandan.

The third one is a swinging motion and uppercut with the backfist, an uraken like movement 6 of Empi. The swinging motion sometimes comes over the opponent's head or goes to the side of the opponent's temple. In the swinging up uraken, power should be taken out of the wrist so the fist can snap better and connect at the end. Be careful not to snap or hyperextend your elbow in the uraken. Your strength is generated by the rotating motion of the hips and goes into the attack at the moment you touch the opponent. Without the hip rotation the technique will not work.

There are two different motions you can use to attack the opponent with uraken, especially when the attack comes from the first and second directions:

First, move in with a sliding motion. For example, if your left side is to the front, just slide the left leg forward and at the same time execute the left hand uraken. Second is stepping in. With the left side forward, step forward like oizuki and execute uraken with the right hand. With this type of uraken your hips are not thrusting. It looks like a thrust but at the last moment you are swinging the hips. So in a realistic case, it's very effective because your opponent expects a thrusting technique. As you step, you have to be aware of your other hand and cover your weak points against the opponent's thrusting attack when you are inside the ma (distance).

You must also practice hitting exact vital points with the uraken, not just the shoulder or the chest. You have to hit the target, so you have to practice until you are accurate. A generally accepted rule for uraken and other techniques is to apply them from a hard part of the body to a soft part or vice versa.

Seniors should be careful when teaching uraken so that juniors don't injure their fists or elbows. Emphasize using the forefinger and middle finger knuckles of the fist for the striking area when using uraken, not those of the ring and little finger. Don't hit with the wrist or the back of the hand. Also don't hyperextend the arm so that the elbow goes completely straight.

Remember, too, that even though you are touching with the back of the first two knuckles, you still have to tighten your small finger very strongly, otherwise the uraken won't work. And also, you have to make a solid form of the fist at the last minute when you touch the opponent and keep the correct form of the wrist.

Your arm and shoulder have to be very relaxed. When you swing a stick, it's not very effective. But tie a stone or iron ball on a string and swing it and it becomes a deadly weapon. So take the power completely out of the shoulder and arm until the last minute. Let the forearm be like the string and the hand like the iron ball. At the last minute, tighten your wrist and fist, but still have no conscious power in the arm, and connect with the rotating hips. This rotation of the hips is the key. You can feel uraken, coming from the hips, become very effective. When you execute, no matter what direction, this fist connects with the hip's movements through the underarm. Make sure you practice uraken on a makiwara or hitting a bag, using the swinging motion to see how this connection is made.

All effective, efficient techniques in combat require mind and body to go together, not only in feeling but also timing, combined with the power of execution and dynamic movement. Until everything is one, we have to practice. In uraken that means making sure that no parts of the body are moving against the direction of the technique.

When you practice tobikomi uraken, jumping in with backfist, you stand with one leg, connecting the back leg to the hip and connecting the hip to the backfist. In this way, even though one leg is in the air, the uraken is still effective.

In Heian Nidan, there is a place (movements 7 and 8) where you stand with the left leg and pull both fists to the left hip and then make uraken at the same time with a right side up kick. Although this is not a realistic motion, there is the meaning to develop a strong stance and stabilize the hips and connect the opposite side underarm with the uraken. This kind of training is very useful for the beginners because they are not really capable of executing uraken or kicks with a strong stance. When beginners first learn these movements, you can tell how long they have practiced. Only people who have trained long enough and whose bodies have started to move can execute it very well. Somebody who has never practiced karate is very awkward. So this very awkward and unrealistic movement has an important purpose for training juniors.

Enpi (Elbow Attack)

Enpi is elbow attack, and some people spell it e–m–p–i like the kata Empi, but the original pronunciations in Chinese were quite different. Although the Japanese islanders pronunciation sounds exactly the same for both, one is enpi, monkey elbow, which means elbow attack technique, and the other is Empi, or flying swallow.

Enpi is one of the most effective and realistic techniques for all members, but especially for the short, light person who doesn't have much power in hand techniques, but who can still make very realistic and effective elbow attacks.

Enpi is a very powerful attack, but it can be very difficult to use in a real situation because its effective distance is short and if your opponent controls your elbow, it is difficult to move well. The elbow is kind of slow to move because the upper arm is not naturally skillful. (The skillful parts are fingers, wrist, forearm, but not the upper arm and shoulder.) Also the elbow is very difficult to connect with your hip movements, so always try to connect it with both underarms, your hips and a strong stance.

This is a very short technique so it's easy to miss with this attack. You've got to make sure you can contact the opponent's body when you execute it. If you use the power even a little too quickly, this blow will not be realistic. So use almost no power, then at the last minute feel strong, when the unconscious power penetrates with the elbow. We should all practice enpi until we are confident that, even against bigger, experienced opponents, we can make a realistic technique.

Here is one good way to practice enpi. From natural stance step back with the right leg into back stance and execute an elbow attack to the rear. Next step forward into front stance and execute enpi upward to the jodan level under the opponent's chin. Then without altering the stance, strike downward with the elbow as if you were attacking the opponent's chest or the back of his neck. This is a useful technique if the opponent bends down, leaving the back of his neck exposed. After this attack, swing the elbow to the left and finally swing it back to the right.

After practicing these five basic elbow attacks with the right side, perform the same sequence with the left side. In this manner you can cover all the basic elbow techniques. Be careful not to put conscious power in your shoulders or arms. Rather, connect your elbow to your underarms and to your hip movements.

You can learn enpi in a short period of time. If you do this technique maybe 10,000 or 20,000 times, you can use it effectively. In other words, compared with oizuki or gyakuzuki, where it can take a million times to bring you some realistic sense and effectiveness, with just 10,000 enpi you can reach a good level.

Bari-Bari, Renzuki (Multiple Attacks)

Bari-bari or renzuki means multiple punch attacks from one stance.

Traditionally, bari-bari was made standing in kibadachi, facing straight to the front, attacking with two or more continuous thrusting techniques. This was a training method of Shotokan groups for many years. When they punch, both shoulders are straight to the front.

I now give this practice of making bari-bari to the front with a wide kibadachi a big question mark. When you are facing straight with a wide kibadachi stance, your entire centerline is open to the opponent. First, you are showing all of your weaknesses to the opponent. No matter how you attack, you always risk getting a kick to the groin. Second, neither of the attacking hands has any kime (focused power). This was not the original, realistic practice.

Originally, in the Okinawan Islands, nobody opened up their centerline and made kibadachi and faced straight and made bari-bari. The last 50 years, careless university students in Japan did this bari-bari with kibadachi. If you decide to make bari-bari from kibadachi, make your kibadachi much narrower. Don't open the knees very much because your opponents can kick you. Consider a realistic situation where you cannot open your centerline to the opponent. Both shoulders stay on the same line, don't move them forward and backwards.

I don't teach bari-bari with kibadachi stance with the legs open to the front any more because it can never be realistic. The bari-bari practice I am emphasizing now uses a stance like the original Hangetsu stance, which comes from the Shokei school. For instance, stand with the right leg back, the toes of the right foot facing straight to the opponent. The left leg is forward, left toe in to cover your centerline and the left knee never opening up to the opponent's front kick. Make both knees solid, very strong both inward and outward, then make your shoulders round from behind — we never make a chicken wing — and then make bari-bari. Each of your attacks has to be powerful and effective with a strong back leg. The heels stay planted and each punch connects with your heel.

Your body is not completely square until you execute gyakuzuki. Then, after you execute gyakuzuki, when your front hand goes in to make maete, your front shoulder also goes forward. Your rear heel stays firmly on the ground and connects with both punching hands.

One good practice is to make three punches at a time: gyakuzuki, maete, gyakuzuki. For this practice your body is square for the gyakuzukis, your front shoulder goes in for the maete. You can alternate making this practice facing front with first the right hand and then with the left hand. With these three continuous attacks, everybody can learn how the fist connects with the back heel and find the correct position of the shoulder.

Kicks and Leg Attacks

I think all of us as human beings, when we are immature or young, usually use legs more than arms when we fight. Later, we learn other techniques, and learn about the natural movements in a fight. But even if we know that we can use the forehead or that we can use both arms, still many of us use our legs because they are long and powerful and we can stay farther away from our opponent. Therefore, kicks come first in karate practice most of the time. So, to train young people in the beginning, I think it's quite normal and natural to include lots of kicks in the practice.

Kicks are a special feature of karate against other martial arts, so our legs have to be strong enough to destroy opponents with kicks or stamps. The strongest part of any kick has to be the standing leg. Whenever you execute a kick, your standing leg supports not only the weight of your whole body but also your opponent's power and weight.

Young people are very enthusiastic and want to use kicking techniques. They have to be careful not to hurt their knees, their ankles, their hips or their backs. Karate practice has to be healthy and strong. Karate practice also has to be realistic and effective and, therefore, you have to repeat techniques over and over. To make even very natural techniques like stamping kick effective may take several years. You have to kick every day over 200 times, maybe 70,000 times a year. That is the minimum actually. To make a kick good and effective, it may take half a million times. But if the kick we are practicing is unhealthy and it starts to hurt some part of our body before we even reach 100,000 times, there is something wrong with that basic training. You have to be very critical of that kind of practice. Artificial movements can cause injury or damage that will last a lifetime. Therefore, teach smooth, healthy kicking techniques.

Emphasize timing and distance when studying kicks against punches. Hand techniques are quicker so when you execute kicks against hand techniques, you have to be very sensitive to the ma (timing and distance). Also be aware of your position and your opponent's position. Keep the ma exact, otherwise there is not much chance of making the kicks work.

Maegeri (Front Kick)

Maegeri is front kick. "Mae" means front and "keri" ("geri") means kick. I think the maegeri movement appeared much later than the stamping or sweeping movements. Compared with these primitive kicks, maegeri is a very sophisticated kick.

We have a million front kicks, each is different. Of course, all have the same basic elements, even when kicking with the toes, heel, shin, etc. These elements are strong standing leg, hips in, upper body calm, and a kicking leg which is free and snaps to the target.

I hope everybody can make maegeri without much trouble. Always think that the mind goes first, body follows second. If you kick without preparing your mind first, you hurt your body. Therefore, we always wake up our minds before we exercise. To be effective, we have to practice maegeri many times.

As with all kicks, we can make maegeri with both the front and back leg. They have different good and bad points.

With rear leg maegeri, we learn big, dynamic motions and practice shifting weight. This is an important training method. You should learn how to shift the hips to the front dynamically, because that makes the human mind courageous. The disadvantage is that when you kick with the rear leg, it's much easier for the opponent to catch the moment when you're starting.

It is much quicker and more realistic if you can kick with the front leg, not only in maegeri, but also with mawashigeri, fumikomi, yokogeri kekomi, any kick. It's much harder for the opponent to see when you begin to kick, but the weakness is the very short distance of the kick. It doesn't have the dynamic movement that kicking with the rear leg has. The motion is so small that if you don't practice it a lot, it is difficult to make an effective kick. If you want to make your maegeri realistic, you should practice many kicks with the front leg.

I suggest this order for practicing maegeri. First we have to learn a big feeling, a big motion; second power and strength; and third, quickness with one motion. This is why we teach front leg kicks after rear leg kicks. After many kicks with a big feeling then some people start to understand, and we teach actual, realistic kicks executed by the front leg. This way people start to understand how to make the short, quick movements with the front leg realistic and effective.

Many parts of the kick are the same regardless of whether you use the front or back leg. With a strong back leg, the front knee goes up and you execute the kick with the upper body leaning into the opponent, not leaning back. If just your leg goes toward the opponent, the kick won't work and you might fall down. And also, when you execute maegeri, be careful to keep the back toes in, not going to the back.

When you make maegeri, the correct foot position for the kicking foot is very important. Many members have a loose ankle on the kicking leg and let the kicking foot drop. If you look from behind the person kicking, you should not see the bottom of his foot as he kicks. When I was a beginner, Senior Watanabe used to put a little matchbox on top of our foot and if we started to kick and the matchbox fell onto the floor instead of going in the direction of the kick, that was wrong. You have to make the correct form with a strong front leg pulling the kicking leg. Don't tense the thigh or calf, just keep the kicking leg kind of loose. Only the ankle is slightly tight so the kicking foot points directly to the opponent. That will increase the speed of the kick.

You have to know how to kick without injuring yourself. Kicks are not all that safe. There is a possibility of breaking your toe or ankle if the kick is done incorrectly. Your breathing has to come to the toe every time when you kick. Your mind and breathing penetrate the target before you touch your opponent.

Of course, any kick has to be connected with all other parts of the body. The kick is done not only by kicking leg. The whole body makes the kick. And the center of the body is the hips, strong and stabilized. When you are supported by a strong standing leg, you can make free, effective kicks. Kick with a strong standing leg and make your standing foot remain motionless for the best possible kick. Kick with one motion and make sure you kick straight to the target.

It is very difficult to stand with one leg against a bigger, tougher opponent. There are two important points. First, you have to execute the right timing. The moment your opponent starts to come, you start to kick. Second, your standing leg has to be solid, because you must keep your balance to support your weight and also your opponent's weight, momentum and power. This takes a strong standing leg.

Many people think that front kick has a very long effective distance. That is not true. The distance is almost the same as the opponent's touching distance. When the opponent can almost get you, this distance is the best time to execute kicking techniques.

We also make maegeri with the front leg in a back stance. To make this kick effective, you must have a strong, connected back leg. The hips should feel like they are moving in. Practice applying this kick after stepping into back stance with shuto-uke. When you kick, don't let your arms fly around.

Maegeri Practice:
One of the hardest parts of maegeri to learn is to kick with a strong standing leg and a standing foot that does not move. If a junior has inflexible ankles, they will tend to make front stance with the back toe and knee pointing to the side instead of the front which means the front kick is often done with the standing leg toe pointed to the side and both knees bent outwards. By raising the heel of the kicking leg and closing the stance as described below, you will get the feeling of a straight kick. The rest of the body should remain as in normal maegeri practice.

To make this practice make a front stance. Move all the weight to the front leg with *no* weight on the back. Move the back foot so only the ball of the foot is touching the floor, the stance is very narrow and the toes and knee of the back leg point exactly forward. Kick in a straight line with one motion. The standing leg does the work. The kicking leg just goes straight through. Make sure the knees pass close together. Do not move the standing foot or let it turn as you make the kick.

This is not a normal maegeri practice, but it can help teach a straight, one-motion kick with a proper standing leg.

Another maegeri practice is to apply all of the elements of maegeri to a realistic situation. You must be free to adjust them as needed. Sometimes quickness gives way for more accuracy. Strength, an all-important element, might give way to a quicker snapping kick used to stop an onrushing opponent while you are backing up. This is the study of maegeri, how it is used for different situations.

Also practice ippon gumite with kicks. Remember toe and instep are vital points. Avoid hurting these parts even when making a realistic practice. For example, don't carelessly block someone's leg with an elbow or kick with no control to someone's ribs. This carelessness must be avoided.

Mawashigeri (Round Kick)

Mawashigeri means round kick. "Mawashi" means round and "keri" ("geri") means kick. Sometimes this is also called roundhouse kick.

Mawashigeri is a very sophisticated, very new technique compared to techniques like fumikomi and uraken. It is a newer variation of maegeri .

These days I like to start with front leg mawashigeri because it makes the kick clearer and you can make this kick with one motion. To make front leg mawashigeri, first make kibadachi correctly, then lift your kicking leg up, keeping the same kind of form in the standing leg. It's like kibadachi in the air, with one leg standing on the ground and the other leg up. For the kicking leg, the ankle and knee have to be horizontal. When you kick, you have to keep both the knee and the ankle horizontal, at the same level and not let them drop. After executing mawashigeri, don't let the kicking leg down before it comes back to the starting position. Many people, after kicking, let the toe down or drop their leg without bringing the kicking leg back first. That changes the position and can cause lower back problems. You have to keep the kicking leg horizontal, before and after you kick and then come back down to the original kibadachi form. This is the form of mawashigeri you should make to avoid hurting any part of the body.

After practicing front leg round kick, you can practice back leg round kick. Beginners have to be careful making round kick because sometimes they twist their hips and upper bodies in opposite directions, making an unhealthy movement that hurts their back, hips, knees or ankles. If you practice the following two instructions carefully, you can avoid unhealthy movements of the hips:

First, your hips rotate with your shoulders. In other words, hips don't go one way and shoulders another, especially in back leg mawashigeri. One way to learn to do this in one motion is to raise both your arms, imagine you have a sword in your hands and then step forward with rotating hips into kibadachi and swing both arms down and across like you are chopping somebody's head off. This movement makes the natural rotation of the hips and shoulders.

Second, right after you execute mawashigeri finish the same way you make front leg mawashigeri. Don't drop your leg down to the ground.

Keep your leg and toes up on the line where you executed the kick, with the knee and ankle horizontal, almost like making kibadachi in the air. Then go back to kibadachi standing on the ground.

The most important point to keep in mind about mawashigeri is connecting all the parts of the body with the rotating hips. All effective, efficient techniques in combat require mind and body to go together, not only in feeling but also timing, combined with the power of execution and dynamic movement. Until everything is one, we have to practice. In mawashigeri that means making sure that no parts of the body are moving against the direction of the technique. Without the correct hip motions, this kick can never be effective.

For many years, I have also emphasized that, when executing mawashigeri, your hips have to pass the line between your standing leg and the opponent's body. Your hips have to pass this line when you kick, otherwise mawashigeri is not completely effective and you cannot make kime (focused power). On the other hand, when you finish your kick, don't expose your back to the opponent's counterattack.

In the beginning, when you are just learning mawashigeri, don't make the kick high or execute it with too much power. Everybody make a slow and careful kick, with the correct form, and then get used to doing it with rotating hips, with knee and ankle horizontal and landing in a kibadachi stance.

To make a realistic mawashigeri with one motion, you have to use your front leg. In combination with some other technique, you can make mawashigeri with the rear leg, but you cannot go in one motion directly from the back leg to the opponent with mawashigeri. To make this kick with one motion, you have to use the front leg.

Yokogeri Keage (Side Up Kick)

Yokogeri keage comes from the Japanese "yoko" meaning side, "keri" ("geri") meaning kick, "ke" meaning kick and "age" meaning up. We usually call this side up kick in English.

Originally, yokogeri keage was the same as maegeri. The only difference between the two kicks is that in side up kick the upper body position is to the side.

As late as the 1950s, ninety percent of Master Funakoshi's pupils were still following the fashion of the 1930s and making yokogeri keage with the side edge of the foot, without turning or opening the hips, something like a cow's kick. I saw that many of them were damaging their backs. After I damaged my back this way, I talked to Senior Obata (one of the original seniors under Master Funakoshi and the first captain of the Keio University Karate Club in the 1930s) when he came to the United States. I told him that I thought there was something wrong with this kick and he agreed with me that this way of doing side up kick was very bad for the lower back. He asked me, do you remember Master Funakoshi's side up kick? Yes, I remember, I told him, and I demonstrated it for him. He insisted that we go back to this original side up kick that Master Funakoshi taught.

These days I'm teaching yokogeri keage to the side. When practicing to the side, you don't need any twisting hip motions. Make the side up kick from kibadachi, almost like a front kick, but without turning the body. Step up with the back leg, knees and feet together, not crossing or stepping to the front or back, but exactly on the line. Practice opening your hips with the front knee going in the kicking direction, then snapping the kick exactly on the line. Keep the standing leg bent during the kick. Then go back to kibadachi. After turning, make the kick again in the opposite direction.

Some people misunderstand and think that yokogeri keage requires a twisting or rotating hip motion, but that is not true. The only kicks requiring this kind of turning hips motion are mikazukigeri (crescent kick) and mawashigeri (round kick). Yokogeri keage should not use any twisting motion of the hip.

Also many people turn their hips and shoulder so they are facing the kicking direction. But, if you turn your hips and shoulder, you are making front kick. Side up kick is executed with both hips and both shoulders on the line. When you are standing in kibadachi facing to the side and turn your hips to make your kick, the front hip goes back. That takes power away from the kick. For side up kick you need to open your hips and keep your knees and shoulders on the line

I hope all my students understand the right way to make this kick and are proud to kick side up kick this way, no matter what other people are doing. All instructors should have confidence in this kick and always emphasize the original side up kick with open hips.

If you have trouble kicking very high, don't worry. Kicking at the opponent's knee level is good enough in the beginning. Then gradually kick higher as you continue to practice.

Yokogeri Kekomi (Side Thrust Kick)

Yokogeri kekomi come from "yoko" meaning side, "keri" ("geri") meaning kick, "ke" meaning kick and "komi" meaning put into or thrust. We usually call this side thrust kick.

I always emphasize that this is one type of fumikomi (stamping). Beginners learning this kick should not try to kick high and should not make fancy, theatrical kicks to show off, because they are not good for your health.

There are many other groups and instructors who are damaging their student's hips and backs because they don't understand the fundamental movements. The basic understanding is that human, healthy movements will not hurt our body, but unhealthy ones will.

Beginners should practice fumikomi first, before attempting yokogeri kekomi. This way they will not take a chance of hurting their spine. After you learn to make fumikomi without any unhealthy movements, you'll find that the feeling is almost the same when you execute a lower level side thrust kick. After you get used to making this kick, even if you can only kick low, find out how to make it realistic and effective.

In the basic kick make sure you make the feeling of knee up and thrusting down. Emphasize a strong ankle and using the side edge or heel of the foot, not the ball of the foot. Always make a strong standing leg. Start with a two motion kick, stepping and then kicking. Then practice to get a one-motion kick where the standing leg lands simultaneously with the foot kicking the opponent. Make one feeling in both legs so the kicking leg connects to the standing leg.

You've got to protect your hip and back when you make this difficult thrust kick. You must move very carefully with a strong thrust motion. Kicking at the opponent's knee level is good enough in the beginning. Then gradually kick higher as you continue to practice. By starting with an understanding of a low kick, you can learn to make a natural, effective, realistic side-thrust kick without hurting your body.

Mikazukigeri (Crescent Kick)

Mikazukigeri means crescent kick. "Mikazuki" means third-day moon (the crescent moon in the third day of the lunar cycle) and "keri" ("geri") means kick.

You must rotate your hips strongly to make this kick work. Without the correct hip motions, this kick will never be effective. Once you learn how to move your hips, this is one of the most powerful kicks and a very natural movement of the human leg. If somebody has powerful legs, this is the kick they should practice.

I don't know why people don't practice mikazukigeri more. Within just a few thousand kicks, you can learn how to make it effective. We should practice this and apply it in sweeping techniques. And it is effective not only in sweeping. You can also destroy your opponent's knee, thigh, stomach or chest.

In the katas we hit our own hand, so sometimes we misunderstand and leave the hips behind. In a real kick we are not hitting our own hand, and we have to rotate our hip completely, past the line between us and our opponent. In the beginning you don't have to kick high. This powerful kick naturally goes higher if you practice it many times.

Fumikomi (Stamping Kick)

Fumikomi means stamping kick. "Fumi" is stamp and "komi" means put into.

Fumikomi is one of the primitive movements that all apes know how to make. Primitive does not mean bad. It means original and realistic. This is the oldest leg attack. We have a document from about 1,200 years ago which describes a fight where Takenouchi Sukune defeated Taimano Kehaya with a throw and a stamping kick to the chest. This used to be a very important fighting technique.

In practicing fumikomi, remember that this is a stamp and not a kick. Many people want to make fumikomi like a side thrust kick, but this is not side thrust kick, it's stamping. Of course, they are related kicks. The side thrust kick is the same as fumikomi, but it is aimed at a higher target. I cannot say at what level fumikomi stops and side thrust kick begins, but when you practice fumikomi, don't confuse it with side thrust kick.

For fumikomi make the strongest stamping form with a strong standing leg, knee up and dynamic execution. You must use a direct movement of the leg, with all your power, all your weight, everything moving down to the earth. The key is the standing leg. So start with a strong standing leg. Then the kicking side's knee goes up to the shoulder on the same side. The foot comes straight down. When you touch the opponent, a solid standing leg connects with the psoas muscle to the kicking leg as you stamp, almost making an arch, all one piece. With the underarm muscles tight, shoulders down, head facing in the opponent's direction, small finger tight and everything coordinated together, penetrate the opponent with the heel and the edge of the foot. Be sure you keep the opposite shoulder down and tighten the opposite underarm.

Once you have learned basic fumikomi, practice turning your hips and making udeuke, getting out from the opponent's strongest focus to the side, then stamp. This is a basic self-defense technique.

Unfortunately, we cannot stamp on the floor of the dojo every time we make fumikomi. If we could do it, in a way it would be more natural. We can do a little more stamping with a fumikomi like the one in Heian Sandan because it is a little different from what we are doing when we make basic fumikomi. Sometimes it's better to touch the ground if we don't hurt our feet or legs or hips. If we always kick in the air, people never realize that when we kick and actually make contact, so much power can come back to our body that the kick doesn't work. On the other hand, if we stamp too strongly every time, it hurts our heels or ankles. Sometimes it may give you even worse trouble. So it is very difficult to determine how much you can and cannot stamp. Find a balance so you don't get injured either way — one, because of not kicking realistically; and two, because of stamping too strongly every time or too many times.

These days I'm teaching fumikomi to the side because originally these kicks were executed from hanmi stance to the side. When practicing to the side, you don't need any twisting hip motions.

We should still practice fumikomi stepping forward and facing to the kicking side, bringing the kicking knee up to the chest before kicking, along with all the other basics. Some instructors misunderstand this practice and are teaching fumikomi starting from zenkutsu dachi. This is incorrect. Start from shizentai, count, step forward and stamp to the side.

When you make the kick, pay attention to these points. Mentally the kick starts even before stepping into zenkutsu. Starting from shizentai and then stepping in is important because it teaches us how to get a *one* feeling. Try to get this *one* feeling without excess arm movements. Weight goes to the kicking leg. Eyes are always eye level in the kicking direction. It is important when kicking that the opposite arm and shoulder do not go up.

If you practice only from zenkutsu dachi, without the stepping motion, it's hard to understand how to connect your standing leg with the stamping leg. Without many repetitions of the correct technique, the kick will not be realistic. In a real situation as an offensive fumikomi you would jump in toward the opponent and, when the standing leg lands, simultaneously stamp. When you use fumikomi defensively, you don't have to jump into the opponent, but you must have a solid standing leg to take his momentum.

This is a very powerful kick, but you have to learn the proper way to kick without hurting your body. I suggest at least 200 fumikomi per day, and within a year your fumikomi will become quite reasonable.

Hiza Geri (Knee Attack)

Hiza geri means knee attack. This is an effective and powerful technique as a counterattack. However, it's very short, so it's easy to miss with this attack. You've got to make sure you can contact the opponent's body when you execute this technique. As with all kihon, you must imagine a realistic situation and the most effective counterattack.

Knees, used correctly, are one of the most powerful parts of the body. But if you use the power just a little too quickly, this blow will not be effective. So use almost no power, then at the last minute feel strong, when subconscious power penetrates with the knee.

Don't try high attacks with the knee. Attack the lower parts of the body, the opponent's shin or knee from the side or thigh. That's a knee attack. Until we can use knees freely, we should practice using them, especially when facing larger opponents, always attacking vital points.

Front Leg and Jumping Kicks

I'm expecting everyone to practice front leg kicks and jumping kicks which are very realistic and effective close to the opponent. In real combat your rear leg attack takes a long time and cannot catch the opponent, so your front leg kicks have to work. It is important to be realistic when you practice kicks kumite and kihon.

When you make jumping kicks, hips and head don't go up, especially when you first start to jump in. You have to give the opponent the impression you're coming in at eye level, while jumping in deep, otherwise you cannot reach the opponent. When you land, it's much more effective if your landing and kick are simultaneous.

Usually we think about jumping kicks from kibadachi or front stance but you can also make jumping kick from back stance. Start with a strong stance. Bend your ankle and knee, keep your hips low and your front leg free to make a strong kick. From here, practice jumping in when you kick and land simultaneously with your back leg on the floor. If you practice it many times, you can make this kick very quickly, with one motion. Your opponent will find it very difficult to see when you are starting and you will have a chance to get him.

Since the kick only travels a short distance, it's very difficult to knock out someone with one kick, so be sure to continue with a front hand jab or a backfist attack. Follow that immediately with a gyakuzuki with the other hand or another technique. Practice this combination kick with front or rear hand techniques continuously until you can execute it without thought.

Zuzuki (Head Attack)

Zuzuki means head attack. We don't generally practice this as a basic but it can be quite realistic. Members who want to pick this technique as a favorite should find out a system to improve this basic. However, I don't suggest that you practice head attack like some stupid guys who hit a hard wall or tiles with their forehead, because you can get brain damage.

Combinations

When we work on combinations, the emphasis is on effective techniques executed continuously. All of us have to think of the realistic situation, what it is and what kind of elements we need to understand. The most important is to make each technique realistic, effective and efficient, with a very free feeling that allows us to adjust to the situation. We also have to consider coordination and balance.

In the beginning you should practice a block and attack or two attacks making sure that both techniques are effective. Keep the conscious power out of your shoulders. Concentrate on getting your mind and body together on both techniques to make the most effective kime (focus of power). Don't make your first attack weaker on continuous attacks. You should try to damage your opponent on the first attack, then follow through exactly with the next. Each technique should be effective enough to stop the opponent's fighting ability. If a technique isn't going to work, it's better not to execute it.

Execute combinations with one feeling, one breathing. Your mind must penetrate the opponent continuously, no matter how you step or attack or block. Don't disconnect your feeling or breathing in front of your opponent.

Always make your combination attacks using your own unique movements, realistic techniques that you like, and then repeat them many times continuously. Make these techniques your own strength and secret weapon. It's important to understand that combination techniques are very individual choices, because everybody has a different nature, a different figure and different physical abilities. So you can do what you think is best for you. Usually we emphasize two or three attacks, but we always have to consider realistic combat at any level. We have to know what techniques we can depend on, right now, at this level.

Blocks and Counterattacks

The block, by itself, is not enough in karate. Sometimes a block becomes a counterattack, but there are always two elements in one.

Sometimes different hands and different techniques go together, but the block and counterattack are always one feeling, one breathing, one timing.

To make an ideal counterattack, you must make a strong block and both must be one unit. To accomplish this, you must feel as one. Breathing must be one and you should not cut your breathing between the block and the counterattack. Be aware of your feeling and your breathing while practicing block-counterattack combinations.

Studying blocks with counters is kind of like Ten No Kata, I think. I hope that as people digest the basics they find some favorite counterattacks with some favorite blocks. You cannot be experts in everything from the beginning, but be sure to repeat your favorite block and counterattack until it becomes effective.

Kicks and Punches

All black belts understand consciously, intellectually, that when you kick, you should not open your upper body or face, and that when you punch you should not show weakness in the lower parts. But when we execute one thing, we sometimes forget about the other parts.

When you kick, you have to cover your face. When you punch, you have to cover the lower parts of your body. We can only have the ability to do this in a real situation by repeating combination techniques many times. Every time you attack with the right hand, the left hand covers the face and you're ready to kick. When you kick, be sure that you cover your face every time and can execute any block or any attack with either hand continuously after the kick.

Bari-bari (multiple punches) after maegeri is a practice we sometimes make. Make the kick. When you land make bari-bari. When you get close to your opponent, your hips have to go down. If you immediately execute two, three or four continuous attacks, this is not so bad.

Another reason for combinations is that some attacks are very hard to do by themselves. For example, an elbow attack is very difficult to execute from a far distance, but by kicking first, you can get in close and then execute enpi.

Maegeri – Maete (Front Kick – Jab)

In the martial arts, we try to fully utilize all of our advantages over our opponent. The closest distance to the opponent is the front foot and front hand.

Make a coordination of the legs and arms when you kick and punch with maegeri-maete. Don't make it two separate motions, especially in your breathing. Right after you kick, don't stop and then punch. Before the kicking leg lands, right after you finish the front kick, already start your maete with hips continuing in.

You should practice the following points. Learn to use the focus of the body as well as the hands and feet. The direction of the body must be a straight line to the opponent. All unnecessary motions which telegraph your intentions to the opponent must be eliminated. The idea is to get to the opponent in one motion.

Yokogeri Keage – Uraken (Side Up Kick – Back Fist)

Yokogeri keage – uraken is something like movements 6 and 9 in Heian Yodan. For beginners it's very difficult to do, but it's very good practice for developing a strong one-leg stance and also for tightening the opposite underarm. In other words, if you execute uraken with the right arm, keep the left shoulder down and left fist pulled to the hip, and then tighten the left underarm. This makes the kick and uraken effective.

Yokogeri Kekomi – Uraken (Side Thrust Kick – Back Fist)

This is a very realistic set of moves which was a favorite of early Shotokan practitioners both in Japan and in the United States. This pair of techniques is especially effective because the side thrust kick can attack several different targets from the foot to the head and is effective from a range of distances. The timing of the back fist can also be adjusted to fit the actual situation.

Shuto-uke – Nukite (Sword Hand Block – Spear Hand Attack)

We emphasize the stance, back stance and front stance and then shifting hips back to front, front to back. You have to continue practicing moving your hips, and try to reach the level where your hips follow your strongest feeling.

Shuto-uke and nukite are both open hand techniques so you must learn how to use open hand techniques without breaking your fingers. The important things are the position of the thumb and making your feeling come to your fingers. Before attacking or blocking, don't extend your fingers all the way and lock your joints — then you hurt your joints. Actually, the joints are bent a little bit, yet full of feeling. Full of feeling means that when you exhale it feels like your breath is coming out through your fingers.

Mawashigeri with Uraken or Gyakuzuki (Round Kick with Back Fist or Reverse Punch)

The strength of mawashigeri comes from the strong rotating hips. Remember that your upper body does not go the other direction. Hips and upper body go together. Keep your balance and, when you finish the kick, don't expose your back to the opponent's counterattack. Right away, execute uraken or gyakuzuki. You can only do this with a strong, rear-leg stance.

Shuto-uke – Maegeri (Sword Hand Block – Front Kick)

The reason we practice making maegeri immediately after executing shuto-uke is to learn to stand strongly with the back leg and to kick with the front leg.

I suggest that you practice not only going straight back with the shuto-uke and then kicking, but also practice jumping back at a forty-five degree angle. Emphasize the position of your back leg and foot. Land in kokutsu-dachi with your back toe in and heel out and with a strong back leg. Don't let your toe go out — it should almost face the direction of the kick. Maegeri should be executed as soon as the back leg lands. To kick properly, you must stand with a strong back leg and the front leg should be free.

This practice helps us to understand how to make a strong back stance and a free front leg. These principles can be applied to maegeri from front stance also. Kick with a strong standing leg and make your standing foot remain motionless for the best possible kick.

Udeuke — Fumikomi (Forearm Block – Stamping Kick)

This move is very similar to the move we find in Bassai. In Bassai (movements 18 and 19), both hands are open, but this is the same circular motion with your hips, and can be done with udeuke. This is one of the most effective self-defense techniques against a big opponent.

Turn your hips either way, to the right or left, but don't shift your weight onto the back leg. Your hips have to go forward and into the opponent because you're eventually going to stand with the front leg and make fumikomi with the back leg. Sometimes we make a fist, sometimes open hands grab the opponent's arms or shoulder, before we execute the fumikomi.

The kicking leg has to come up close to your body, all the way to your chest, because the opponent's body is very close. Your standing leg is a key. You have to make a very strong standing leg and direct power to the opponent so that you don't lose your balance when you are standing on one leg. When you execute the kick, your breathing always goes through the kicking leg to the edge of the foot where it touches the opponent's body. You must always be conscious of your opponent's pushing power and not lose your balance.

Continuous Kicks

When you're young your legs should be well-trained and you should be able to kick with either leg, any technique, and continuously attack the opponent. This is very powerful when you can use your kicks continuously. Therefore find out how many effective kicks you can execute with one breath. Then later on you can make many different combinations and try to kick continuously.

All young healthy members should train with continuous kicks. I encourage young people to make ten kicks with one count. This way you can learn how to stabilize your hips and make a strong standing leg. Your speed will increase by taking power off right after the kick. With maegeri you pull the kicking leg back right away so it becomes a strong standing leg, and the new kicking leg becomes very light. No power, just speed going into the opponent. You should make other kicks, too, ten techniques with a continuous feeling toward your opponent. That is continuous kick. One breathing, ten kicks.

Of course, you always have to be careful not to hurt your own body. After you start to feel very comfortable with your legs, you must practice how to control you kicks in practice so that you don't hurt yourself or your opponent with your powerful kicks and so that you can both continue to practice for many years.

Tobikomi (Jumping In)

Tobikomi comes from the words "tobi" which means jump and "komi" which means get into. When we talk about tobikomi techniques such as tobikomi oizuki, we mean techniques that cover much more distance than the regular stepping technique would cover.

In the Shorin school, they practiced with much wider stances and a long ma (distance) so they needed to jump in. However, I think the jumping in techniques really started when karate went to Tokyo from the Okinawa Islands. Many people who had practiced kendo came to learn karate and brought their understanding of jumping in techniques with them. This was especially true when they practiced in the dojos where there were flat, wooden floors that made it much easier to jump in from a far distance and then attack the opponent. Before that, there were jumping techniques, but not really tobikomi going *into* the opponent. At Waseda University in the 1930s and 1940s, people did lots of these techniques.

These techniques are disappearing these days because competition has very limited space and you cannot jump in very far. But if you use tobikomi techniques in a very big place when you face opponents, they are very effective. We should keep these traditional Shotokan specialties.

Tobikomi is an expression of a very powerful, extensive feeling towards the opponent. The ability to jump high or far is not worth anything if you do not have a courageous and strong mentality against the opponent. Without that feeling, you cannot make tobikomi. With a penetrating mentality the hips will shift naturally towards the opponent as he tries to escape. Without the penetrating feeling, the opponent just has to move out of the way, and your attack will miss. Therefore, always make tobikomi practice with a strong, penetrating feeling.

In tobikomi each individual also has to get the sense of timing and distance. Jumping *in* is not jumping *up*. The point is, without timing, rhythm and tempo, jumping in techniques don't work. Especially, don't let your head bob up and down and then jump in, because nobody will wait for you.

Your eyes should be level with your opponent's when you get in, and usually we anticipate the opponent's kick or punch, so your middle and upper level have to be covered by arm or knee. When we do tobikomi techniques stepping in, the standing leg has to be very powerful — in a way kind of sticky, holding the body just a little longer — and at the last minute pushing your hips into the opponent.

Emphasize the way you jump into the opponent. Your hips do not go up. The knee goes up to hide your whole middle section. Hand attacks have to connect with dynamic hip movements. To be effective consider at least these points: fist, hips and standing leg have to be one. It's not necessary to stand with two legs, but at least one leg must be connected with the fist and hips.

When you make a jumping in kick, don't use the rear leg to kick. Instead, as you land with the rear leg, simultaneously kick with your front leg (maegeri or yokogeri). This timing can be difficult but it is important to practice until you get it. You can practice kicking a light sandbag, but don't hurt your toes. The first time be careful. Slowly touch the bag and get used to it. Then you can start to increase the power as you kick more.

When you are young, you should practice very dynamic jumps. Young people should know how to make these jumping-in techniques, and everyone should know how they will manage if an opponent comes with jumping-in techniques.

Ukemi (Falling Techniques)

Before we practice ashibarai (sweeping techniques) or nagewaza (throwing techniques) we have to learn ukemi (falling techniques). You should learn how to fall without hurting yourself, your head, your shoulder, your back, your hip, your leg, and you should not get a shock when somebody throws you. You should land safely and be able to face opponents with a continuous mentally.

Even experts, if they don't make ukemi regularly, will panic when they are thrown and land with their face up and their back on the floor. It's more than physical damage. The mental shock is even bigger. Therefore, we should get used to it.

There is nothing wrong with being thrown. It is not the end of the fight. If somebody throws you, with no mental blocks, just get up and continue to fight. Or you can fight on the ground. No matter what position we are in, we should still have many techniques to destroy the opponents and be able to continue.

We always have to prepare our mind that way. Even if the opponent is an expert in throwing, the karate practitioner should have no mental blocks. Always try to imagine the real situation and when, how and what kind of techniques or movements you could use to destroy this opponent.

In many martial arts, especially judo, we learn to fall before we learn how to throw. This is important. Before we hit somebody, we have to know how it feels to be hit. I think this order makes sense. Without learning ukemi, you'll never be able to understand throwing or sweeping techniques.

If there is a judo-ka among your group, it's a very good thing to ask him how to make ukemi properly without any accidents, and then make many ukemi practices.

When we learn ukemi, we practice three basic ways to fall that come from judo. The first way is to squat with your heels up, then fall backward, bending your head forward, rounding your back and hips and, while landing, slap the floor with the palms of the hands to absorb the shock.

The second way is to lie on your back, bend and lift your left knee, crossing it over your right leg and roll sideways. The bottom of your left foot lands flat on the floor to the right of your right knee. Simultaneously, the right palm and forearm slap the floor to absorb the shock. Roll to the left in a mirror image and continue alternating from side to side. Lift your hips farther off the floor as you understand this ukemi better.

For the third ukemi, stand with your right leg a half step in front of the left then bend forward, putting your right hand between your feet, roll forward, pulling your chin to your chest, and land with the bottom of your right foot, left palm and forearm slapping the floor as in the second technique. Keep the left leg slightly up to avoid bruising your ankle. You should roll on the floor with the right arm, behind the right shoulder, angled along the back to the left hip and then to the left leg and right foot. Alternate sides in a mirror image. If this is done correctly, you will not hurt your head, neck or back.

Don't practice ukemi on the hard floor over and over, or you will hurt yourself. Even just a little crack in the spine may never heal properly. Therefore, ukemi has to be practiced in a judo dojo or with a mat, and very carefully. The bone behind the neck and all the bones in the spine are very easily hurt. So when we make any practice with falling, we have to be careful.

Make sure everyone knows how to fall, how to be thrown correctly before you practice throwing.

Ashibarai (Sweeping Techniques)

"Ashi" means leg, "barai" means sweep so ashibarai means leg sweep. In these techniques you are sweeping using rotating hips to unbalance the opponent.

As I am always saying when I talk about this technique, before we practice ashibarai, we have to learn ukemi, falling techniques. Both attacker and blocker have to know how to land safely. When somebody sweeps you, try not to resist and fall down very safely. Then both of you can practice. When you resist, then both sides can get injured.

Ashibarai, which is used a lot as a tournament technique to destroy the opponent's balance, is realistic and effective. As a continuous technique, make ashibarai, sweep the opponent's leg and then, while the opponent is busy trying to restore his balance, execute the next technique. Or you can sweep the opponent and take him to the ground. The moment the opponent gets the shock from the ground, execute your strongest technique.

Even though most throwing techniques have disappeared from karate matches, ashibarai is still popular. This is because we can do it even without holding the opponent's body. It's much easier to control the opponent's front arm with our front hand, then sweep with the front leg or go in deeper and sweep either of the opponent's legs with our rear leg. Or from a far distance, we can jump in unexpectedly, throw our body and swing our leg, hitting the opponent's front or back leg. Just don't underestimate your opponents. If they are a judo-ka or wrestler, we have to respect their specialty. Against this kind of opponent our punches and kicks are more effective. If you get into a grappling match, a judo-ka or wrestler can nail you down very easily.

When you practice sweeping techniques, it is important to avoid injuries. Not only the side being swept, but also the sweeping side can hurt his feet, ankles and knees. If you hurt these parts, you cannot continue to practice. Therefore, first be aware that you should not allow any accident or injury in this practice. If you start to hurt each other, you have to stop right away because you are doing something wrong.

Don't just hit the opponent's ankle or legs or knees without thinking. You should practice with the bag first. Make many repetitions of different types of sweeps before attempting them on an opponent.

With an opponent, begin with very careful movements and only after warming up, when you know where you are touching. Then, just little by little, increase the speed and power. Do not attempt to sweep with your leg. Instead, sweep with the power of the hips behind the leg. The hips have to get in deep. A general rule is to sweep your opponent's leg in the direction their toes are pointing. A hundred times, just touch lightly. Then once, using a mat for protection, use more power. The opponent should not resist too much when his legs are swept and should fall safely. This way we can avoid all injuries and accidents.

Nage No Kata (Throwing Forms)

In nage no kata, nage means throwing, no means of and kata means form so this means practicing the forms of throwing. We also talk about nagewaza which are throwing techniques.

We practice nagewaza because originally we had it as part of our practice. Then, in the middle 1920s when karate went to Tokyo, it began to disappear from Shotokan and other karate schools for quite a long time because karate practitioners were hesitant to use throwing techniques against wrestlers or judo-ka. For fighting against judo, karate throwing techniques are not strong enough, not refined enough, not realistic enough.

From the first, Master Funakoshi did not teach much about throwing techniques, because half of Master Funakoshi's students were judo experts, so they already knew how to throw other people.

When I was nine years old, I started in judo. The whole first year was only ukemi or landing. Every day, just landing practice. That was first. Therefore, I emphasize that before you can learn how to throw, you have to learn how to be thrown. In real combat, as a fighting technique, we have to know how to react and how to protect ourselves when somebody throws us. Also, if we get a chance, we can throw our opponent. Remember, however, that most throwing techniques in karate are against karate people coming to punch or kick. We have to be careful who we use our throwing techniques against because wrestlers and judo experts are so much better. We should be humble when we face these opponents, and use our favorite techniques, strikes or kicks, against them.

When you make throws, use your opponent's power and momentum. This is not some mechanical routine. If you get the right timing and the right position, you can throw the opponent using his energy.

And one other thing, don't forget that throwing itself is not enough. Every time when you throw, you have to execute a kick or punch immediately and make sure you destroy the opponent. Never stop after just a throw and go on to the next opponent because your opponent may not be hurt by your throw and can come back and attack you again.

Kime (Maximum Focus of Power)

Kime is a very vague word for most of us. These days many people stop training before they accomplish kime. Tournament fighting does not require participants to polish their most effective punches and kicks. However, if karate practitioners want to learn how to make their most effective techniques, from beginning to end, they must honestly seek the best way to execute each and every one.

Make it clear, no matter how we move, how we block or execute our techniques, that if it is not strong enough to destroy our opponent, that is not karate. We are always looking for our best, most effective, most realistic, most efficient technique, using our energy in the point, in the moment. We call that kime.

Of course, kime cannot be tested on the opponent's body, so talking about it in this way may seem contradictory. But in karate practice, we have a tradition of understanding that if somebody has kime in their practice, we can tell. So when we practice, I ask everybody to think, "What is kime? How can we get there? How can we evaluate and know if that is kime or not?" Even though I explain the concept with words, you still have to find it in your practice by yourselves.

Kime means maximum effectiveness, your strongest focus toward the opponent. Your total concentrated energy penetrates into or explodes onto the opponent. Between katas and real combat, there are millions of ways of training, strategies or techniques, but to reach the highest level in the martial arts you have to get the understanding of kime.

There are four elements, four gates of kime.

First, there is a difference of weight and size. When a huge person attacks a very small person, that destroys the opponent completely.

Second, there are the vital points. Even a lousy technique, if it hits an opponent's vital point exactly, can have maximum effectiveness and cause the opponent to fall down or die. You must hit these points exactly. Smaller, lighter people must learn to attack these vital points, especially in kumite, but with control. To practice this gate, I suggest that you make a small target, about the size of a thumb nail, and strike it with your fist, knuckle, fingers or toes. This is one way to practice hitting vital points.

Third, is the situation where you attack emptiness with fullness. Emptiness means old or sick, or very depressed emotionally, or the moment in your breathing when you start to inhale after exhaling. Fullness is your youth, your health, your very positive attitude and the time when you are exhaling. At this moment of fullness against an opponent's emptiness, you can have tremendous effectiveness.

Fourth, is the technical viewpoint. If you are completely concentrated, if you have become one and executed your best form, with no wasted energy, with refined technique, even if you are smaller than your opponent, even if you are missing vital points or are not completely full against your opponent's emptiness, if you make this most refined technique, you can destroy the opponent. This technical viewpoint, the fourth gate, is what we are practicing most.

These are the four gates of kime. If you have all four together, it is overkill. With just two of the four it is no problem to destroy opponents. Even a small person can defeat a big guy by hitting the exact vital point with ideal breathing and technique.

Sport karate practice hasn't emphasized kime because people are practicing just to make a point. When we practice a technique, it has to have kime. When you execute this way, your finest technique with your strongest energy does not just touch a spot. It penetrates the opponent.

This study of kime was the most important part of karate practice for many centuries. The goal was a single, ideal technique, one punch or kick, that would destroy the opponent completely. In a real situation it's not that easy to do, but when we practice, we always aim to the best in best, the most realistic technique which has kime. This is the most important element of karate practice. Without kime, there is no karate.

Practicing Techniques to the Side

We have been practicing gedan barai or gyakuzuki or oizuki to the side since about 1986 and after five or six years I saw that people were starting to move very naturally, smoothly and quickly with effective hip movements. We introduce this practice-to-the-side to junior members so they can learn to make solid movements to the side while learning the form of the basics. Then after learning moving to the side very well, they can make the same form stepping forward.

Centuries ago, some genius found these ideal, final forms and developed training methods and techniques to reach these forms from natural stance or front stance or kibadachi. I think this shows a very scientific and advanced understanding. Therefore, I emphasize these practices to the side, such as gedan barai or maete-zuki, to make it easy for everybody to make this ideal final form.

No matter whether you are blocking or attacking, or whether you are making oizuki or gyakuzuki, we emphasize three points: first, make one movement without any minor movements; second, move your hips dynamically; third, make a strong back leg. These very important elements make your techniques effective because your mind and body movements become one.

I have found that people can move their hips to the side much more easily than stepping forward. I want to see all beginners connect the mind and the fist and the hips together. The mind goes first, the breathing follows your mind, then the body goes. With this method we can find out how we are unconsciously turning instead of opening the hips. Turning hips and opening hips are not quite the same. It is much easier to open the hips while stepping to the side.

From shizentai (natural stance), step directly to the left or right with opening hips and make your technique. The important point in this practice is that the mind has to lead the body. Without first feeling or imagining an opponent to the side, your movements cannot be strong or quick or powerful. The mind goes first and the body follows. Therefore, start by imagining opponents to the side and always penetrate realistically with one motion. Be sure not to inhale just before you start to move.

The body, fist and hips simultaneously move together with the pulling hand to reach the final form of the technique. To step forward is much harder, much slower. Because most techniques have to be on the line of the body, it is very useful to first teach moving to the side.

I think this method makes it very easy for everybody to make the final, ideal form and make it with the right mentality, the quickest motion and without any minor movements. This move to the side is now a special feature of our basic practice. I hope everybody likes to do it.

Kumite (Sparring)

Kumite is sparring, fighting against an opponent. In Japanese kumite means cross arms, so it means we train each other. That is an important element to realize, we don't make a sparring practice just for ourselves. We do it to learn from each other.

This respectful mentality is first. In kumite, we start with rei and end with rei. We bow to show our respect for our opponent before and after each match. At the beginning of each match, to make it clear why we are sparring, we ask our opponent to please teach us. At the end we thank our opponent for the match. This is our practice. Sincerely, we show our respect for our opponents and make our most honest sparring. This mental preparation must be made before you face each opponent.

Because we have this mentality, there are two important elements in our kumite practice. The first element is to keep as much of a realistic feeling and sense as we can so we can learn how to face real attacks. The second element is to avoid damaging each other in practice so we can continue to practice long enough to learn. Although these two elements may seem contradictory, we still have to keep them both in mind whenever we make kumite.

There are several things that we do to make a realistic feeling. From the moment when we bow to our opponent, we don't show our teeth — that is a Japanese saying which means that we don't smile and we don't laugh when we face each other. Both sides keep a serious attitude. Someone with serious eyes is coming with an attack. You've got to keep serious eyes and make a strong counterattack. If someone is being silly or hoping for a weak attack, there is a much greater danger of someone getting hurt. The worst case is when one opponent is serious and the other is not. The best matches come when both opponents respect the other. Then the attacker can make powerful, realistic attacks and the defender can block or avoid the attack and make realistic counterattacks.

In many of our sparring practices, such as sanbon gumite, we declare exactly which attacks we are going to use. When our opponent knows the attacks, we can make them as strong as possible and as quick as possible with solid basic stances. With this basic practice we can avoid accidents and still practice strongly. Think about your own practice and how much more you wake up when you face someone who is making his attacks for real.

The way we protect our opponents, strange as it seems, is also through this feeling of mutual respect. When you respect your opponent, you can protect him with your strong mentality. We don't practice so we can hurt our opponents or prove that we are superior or show off our level. This is not respect. This is a selfish, immature desire to show how tough we are. Throw that feeling away. If you keep it, then people will get hurt or quit before they can reach a good level. Instead, we have to keep our promise not to damage each other. We know when an attack would have destroyed our opponent without actually having to knock him out. We know that hitting an opponent who is very much our junior doesn't mean we are tough. We know that we aren't allowed to hit on a counterattack, because our opponent, our friend, is making a technique that leaves him open to the counterattack so we can practice strongly.

That is why we practice kumite with our friends with a sincere mentality and strict manners. When we make kumite, we practice preparing our minds in front of an opponent. We are practicing for real, and also we are protecting each other with a spirit that is always realistic and strong. We are polishing ourselves so that in the future we can handle an emergency situation with a calm and courageous mind.

We practice several different type of kumite, basic practices such as sanbon gumite and ippon gumite and more advanced practices such as jiyu kumite and jiyu ippon gumite. It is important to understand why we do each.

Ten No Kata Ura: This is a very basic understanding of sparring with one specified block. It is a controlled form of basic ippon gumite.

Sanbon Gumite: In sanbon gumite (three time sparring), we are facing an opponent's continuous attack, which is his continuous strong feeling to get us. We study how to make our mind stronger than our opponent's. We watch our opponent carefully and then get out from the opponent's attack with our strong mentality. After the opponent's third attack, we focus on making our strongest counterattack.

Basic Ippon Gumite: In basic ippon gumite (basic one-time attack), we learn about the important elements between opponents in combat. We start to move with our opponent's movements, and we move to a better position with a stronger stance than before. After we move, our opponent should be in a weaker position, not a stronger one.

Jiyu Kumite: Jiyu kumite (free sparring) is an advanced practice second to jiyu ippon gumite.

Jiyu Ippon Gumite: Jiyu ippon gumite (free one-time attack) is the most realistic kumite practice. In this practice we learn to read our opponent's mind, to find out the best sense of timing and distance, what is the best strategy and the most realistic, effective attack or block and counterattack under the pressure of the opponent's strongest attack.

Instructors must be careful to make a bridge between basic training and combat when teaching juniors. The first year of a junior's practice should be devoted to making basics and katas with a strong, realistic sense, feeling an imaginary opponent at all times and making basic sparring practices to help clarify the meaning of the other practices. Later the junior should be allowed in serious jiyu kumite but only if he has developed a good foundation. If juniors are allowed to do free sparring too soon, they will not only be likely to hurt themselves physically, but will limit their capacity to reach a higher level.

Other practices such as sitting form, iai, torite, irimi and nagewaza are to learn specific lessons about facing opponents which are appropriate for senior black belts.

We also practice attacks to different levels when we are sparring. Middle level attack is from the tanden (lower abdomen) to the upper chest. Usually we aim for the solar plexus in the front. If the opponent is turned to the side, there are several vital points in their ribs we can attack. In the back, the kidneys are a good middle level target.

Upper level means from the nose to the throat. Don't attack above eye level. The attacker's fist is just above shoulder height, so that we can attack the center of the opponent's chin, or just a little bit higher or lower. That is upper level.

I hope all practitioners will feel no fear about sparring some day, even in front of the toughest opponent. But if you feel uncomfortable, if you feel fear, that's quite normal. That's because you are a human being. Still you have to set a target that someday you will penetrate your fear. Your opponent is right in front of you. Your difficulty is always right there, and the only way to penetrate it is to decide strongly not to turn your head away or close your eyes. From beginning rei to ending rei, you watch your opponents eyes. This training is the only way to get out from the fear.

You have to make a habit to face your opponents straight. Always make your strongest gyakuzuki or other counterattack. You have to practice one favorite technique many thousand times until you feel you can depend on this technique and feel that you can do something no matter what kind of opponent you are facing. Then you can reach the point where you feel no fear about sparring.

Ten No Kata Ura (Form of Heaven Application)

Ten No Kata Ura uses the blocks from Ten No Kata against a real opponent. This is like ippon gumite with a set block and counterattack.

We make this practice with commands from the leader. On the command yoi, both sides make natural stance facing each other at the proper distance. On the command kamaete, the attacker puts the right foot back, making front stance. The blocker remains in natural stance. On the command hajime or with a count, the attacker makes an oizuki at the appropriate target. The blocker makes a block and counterattack according to the kata. On the command yame, both sides return to natural stance.

Make exact form with each other. For instance, the attacking side makes basic middle level oizuki clearly. Then the blocking side blocks and counterattacks with one feeling and one breath, controlling the counterattack. Both sides should kiai. The attacker kiais on the attack and the blocker kiais on the counterattack.

This practice should be formal. Face each other exactly. Make exact form. Don't jump around or shuffle your feet. Watch your opponent's eyes at all times. Move only on command. After you do this practice with commands, older members may practice without commands but the practice should still be formal.

Sanbon Gumite (Three Time Sparring)

Sanbon gumite is three real attacks to a specified target followed by the defending side's controlled counterattack.

When we make sanbon gumite, as we do in all sparring, we start with rei. Then move to the proper distance, just at the edge of ma (about one arm's length apart) and face each other in natural stance.

Some people have a habit of measuring the distance by reaching toward the opponent. It's ridiculous to extend your fingers and measure how far away you're standing. That's only for explanation. A real opponent will attack your arm. You have to feel the correct distance instead, just as you would have to do in a real fight.

When you stand facing the opponent in sanbon gumite, you are already at the edge of ma (closest distance), so you can't step forward without attacking. From the ready stance you have to step back with the right leg and make a zenkutsu gedan barai. Don't make it two or three steps — only one clear movement.

The attack in sanbon gumite is three oizuki attacks to a specified target. What we are trying to learn is how to move our hips courageously. That is the important point. Our mentality has to be strong enough to penetrate the opponent, to move our hips directly toward the opponent. These days I see many people making sanbon gumite where the first attack is oizuki, then the second and third are gyakuzuki. That is not sanbon gumite. You must make your hips move in.

If people break the rules for this practice, later on there will be trouble. Therefore, be sure to make sanbon gumite with exact oizuki from a solid stance, one by one, toward the opponent. Keep low hips, make very strong hip movements and try to penetrate your opponent's body with each attack. It's not enough to touch your opponent's skin. Your feeling penetrates all the way through him with your eyes and your hips going to the opponent's centerline and your back leg solid with the foot and toes in. While you keep this feeling, watch the opponent's eyes and execute the punch, stepping with your hips and making a pulling hand all at the same time. The rhythm is one…two-three (two and three are much closer together). It's not one…two…three, all the same rhythm.

Our primary purpose for this kumite is to learn about strong mentality. The whole body and mind must move as one. The attack in sanbon gumite is a basic training for the subconscious mind.

On the defending side, we are facing an opponent's continuous attack, which is their continuous strong feeling to get us. We study how to make our mind stronger than our opponent's, we watch our opponent carefully and then get out from the opponent's attack with our strong mentality. After the opponent's third attack, we focus on making our strongest counterattack. These are the important points of sanbon gumite practice: eyes, position and counterattack.

Eyes mean we maintain eye contact with our opponent, read the opponent's mind and never show any weakness to the opponent. In other words, our mind has to be very strong. We have to get out from our weakness, our cowardice, our stupidity, our blind points, our bad habits which we have unconsciously. To do this, we face a senior who has a strong mentality and compete with this senior's mentality through eye contact. By watching eyes we can see when the opponent decides to attack. Later on, we can feel not only *when* but *how* and with *what*.

Second, we have to keep the correct position relative to our opponent. We have to have a strong stance with strong hips and a strong back leg. Even if the opponent continuously comes to attack, we can evade or block and get out from the attack.

Third we have to be ready to destroy the opponent when he comes with the third attack. If you are only thinking about how to get out, you'll never be on time with your counterattack. You must make the counterattack immediately after or simultaneously with his last attack. The last block and counterattack should be one breathing. Even before we start sanbon gumite, we decide only one thing: to destroy our opponent right after the third attack. Of course, in practice we must also decide to strongly control our counterattack. People who do not have big bodies, especially women, must strike exact vital points when executing an attack or counterattack. A clear counterattack is important because what counts in combat is our decisive mentality, with no hesitation. There can be no minor movements or lack of confidence. Our body shows our mental weakness or immaturity or unclear feeling, so we are practicing to develop our courageous, clean, strong feeling and make a clear and effective counterattack, a simple one, with a solid stance.

We are facing ourselves through our opponent. He is not an enemy but a partner to help us improve our practice, so don't touch your opponent with your counterattack. Even in your attack, if you know you're going to destroy your opponent, you don't have to hit him to prove it. We are not practicing to hurt our opponent, but to bring our best parts from inside. We should appreciate the opponent who can give us this good practice.

One of the best parts of sanbon gumite is that we can make it with real attacks. Since we declare exactly which attacks we are going to make, the defender knows exactly which attacks are coming and the attacker can make his attack as strong as possible and as quick as possible. But from the defender's side, it is essential to get beyond the idea of using a particular block against the opponent's attacks. For example, it is not wise to think, "When my opponent attacks chudan oizuki with the right hand, I will make gedan barai with my left hand." If you always do this, you will develop bad habits and will not be able to block when you don't know what attack your opponent is going to make. This type of thinking will also cause you to make a late counterattack. Even if you know what the opponent is going to do, erase this knowledge from your mind and think only of making a good, strong counterattack

When we look at our opponent, the important point is to find the moment when he decides to come, and we can do that no matter whether the opponent attacks to the face or the stomach. What is important is to be mentally free from your opponent's attack and to read your opponent's mind. Fear makes your body stiff. To be free, you have to have a courageous mind.

We usually do sanbon gumite with a middle level attack because we have big differences between tall and short persons, between heavy and light persons. So there is a big risk of hurting each other if we are not mature enough, if we are not considerate of our friends. But when I was young, we didn't do it middle level, because when you practice upper level all the time, middle level is very easy. And also we did five time engagement matches, not just three times, all upper level. When some senior comes to punch you, you become an expert at escaping from five punches to the face. I don't want to make bigger risks in our practice but you have to realize that there is no difference mentally between upper and middle level. Someday you have to reach that understanding.

Also when I was young, we were never allowed to block from the outside to the inside with tetsui-uke — one, two, three. That was prohibited, but there are some people now doing this. For somebody without any experience, maybe this seems like a good, easy way, but if you get into that habit, you cannot learn other blocks as well. So if you want to use tetsui against the opponent's attack, upper level or middle level, move to the inside. In other words, when the opponent comes with the right hand attack, don't go to the outside, but inside, with the left leg stepping back and the right arm blocking the opponent's right arm.

Sanbon Gumite without Blocks:

Sanbon gumite without blocks can increase your capability in real combat. Instructors should teach this to white belts and brown belts after they stay a few months, but black belts have to do it many times first. This is one example of sabaki, which means evading practice.

Sanbon gumite without blocks works when we read our opponent's mind with eyes that look strongly at our opponent and when we show our most courageous, strongest feeling. We have to do this practice many times. Then our hips start to move freely and naturally, stepping back or stepping in. The idea is not to jump out, to escape with a negative mentality. On the contrary, we maintain a positive mentality, and our mind penetrates the opponent even though the opponent comes to attack us. Then we can get out.

For this practice we cut our arms off, in your mind almost like you don't have any arms. Put your hands behind your body, into the belt and stand in front of the opponent Still you can get out from the opponent's strongest attack.

When the opponent comes to punch your stomach, you try to move your hips and avoid the opponent's punch. Just use your hips and smooth steps with a strong mentality. Never use your hands to block.

You'll be surprised — you can get out. You must see the opponent's decision the moment he starts to come, then you move at the same time, without waiting for the opponent's actual physical movement. Don't jump around; don't move before the opponent decides to come. That means your mind is scared of the opponent and you are jumpy. You've got to calm down and look at the opponent until the moment the opponent decides to come. Then you start to move.

The original practice in martial arts was not just to learn the techniques. We are really searching for our strongest feeling and ideal mentality. This practice emphasizes that facing the opponent is the most important element. This is not technical level or physical strength, but mental strength. If we don't have two arms to block, we really have to concentrate strongly and prepare our mind so that we are alert and can see the opponent and avoid getting hit.

If we wake up our minds and move with our hips, we can get out from an opponent's attack. But if we depend on our hands, then our mind gets weaker and without a strong mentality it is very hard to avoid the opponent's attack without making a mistake.

This point of our practice makes Shotokan different from other groups. Even when we step back or we evade or we get out from an opponent's attack, we don't have a negative mentality. This is a good example to show how our body is directly connected to the deep, subconscious mind.

After you can get out freely from the opponent this way, you get more confidence about sparring and learning regular sanbon gumite is much easier. When hip movements lead, our blocking is much more realistic. Therefore, I encourage you to wake up and learn to evade an opponent's attack without using your hands or arms to block.

Sanbon Gumite with Extra Low Stances:

One month a year, I emphasize making sanbon gumite with extra low stances, with the hips exactly at the level of the knees. If the hips go lower than this, the legs and upper body cannot be connected and become weaker. But I notice that I seldom have to tell people that they are too low. Usually I have to ask them to get lower.

From a realistic viewpoint, this low form is very difficult to make in front of opponents because we cannot move quickly. We make it anyway because most of the time our hips go up when we are afraid. Both fear and the instinct to move quickly make our hips go up. When we practice sanbon gumite with extra low stances, we overcome our fear with a strong mentality, keeping our hips as low as possible. Then, in a real situation, even if the hips come up a bit, they will still be low enough to be strong.

This is not only a physical training, but a mental training as well. Only the person who is practicing with these low stances can show his courageous mind in front of opponents. In combat, the most important element is courage.

Sanbon Gumite from Kibadachi:

We also make sanbon gumite using kibadachi with the counterattack. This is to learn how to move in kibadachi against a real opponent. After many thousands of times we start to understand how we can be a strong human being, as one, with this stance.

When the opponent attacks with oizuki from zenkutsu dachi, the defender may counterattack in kibadachi, moving to the outside or to the inside of the opponent with the left or right leg moving forward or backward. Either way you must feel free to make your strongest stance against the opponent.

When stepping back with kibadachi, if you execute the hand technique while your hips are moving back, it doesn't work. To be effective when you step back, your mind, your hips and all your power and weight must simultaneously focus and shift toward the opponent with the counterattack.

Sanbon Gumite with Udeuke:

I ask senior members to practice sanbon gumite with udeuke as their block. Seniors don't practice much sanbon gumite because they are so used to facing juniors in special training where they feel superior and don't have any trouble. But if they practice using only udeuke against an opponent's middle level attack and later on practice jodan udeuke, they will be surprised at how hard it can be.

Udeuke shows us our blind points, incorrect form and wrong timing. This seems to be some sort of test to show how we are still incomplete. Therefore, try to practice using only udeuke to get out of the opponent's three-time attack. When you block the opponent's chudan attack with udeuke, when you touch your opponent's wrist, your elbow is close to your body and the block connects with the underarm. You need the right timing, and all blocks need the correct position of the elbow and connection with the underarm to be effective.

Kihon Ippon Gumite (Basic One Time Sparring)

Kihon ippon gumite is one real attack from a stationary stance to a specified target followed by the defender's controlled counterattack.

This is one of the safest kumite practices and there is not much chance of being hurt, but that doesn't mean you can sleep or feel comfortable. There are always points to study, something you have to polish to obtain a sense of combat. Everybody thinks this is the safest practice, but you have to tighten your mind and wake up.

When you start the match, make a distance so that the attacker can step forward. Without moving the right leg, the attacker takes one step forward with the left leg and makes a down block in front stance to get into position to make an attack. In this practice we are learning how to judge the distance.

I expect everybody, when they attack, to make a basic, powerful oizuki at the opponent. Both you and your opponent have to appreciate this meeting. Every time, you make your best attack at your opponent for his practice, then your opponent gives you his best attack for your practice. If you don't make a serious attack, your opponent cannot learn.

When you are the defender in basic ippon gumite, you learn about important elements between opponents in combat. You start to move with your opponent's movements and you move to a better position with a stronger stance than before. After you move, your opponent should be in a weaker position, not a stronger one. If you move to a weaker position, you should not have moved.

Also study the two different timings for your block and counterattack because they are the only two ways to counterattack realistically and destroy the opponent. One is a simultaneous block and counterattack. The other is when you block strongly and unbalance the opponent, making a two-motion block and attack with one breathing. This is the only time when you can make a two-motion block and attack, when you have unbalanced your opponent and he cannot move immediately.

In a real situation, the opponent may follow the first attack with a second and a third. If your counterattack is two motions, while you evade the first attack, the opponent can still injure you with his second and third attack. When I say to make your kime (your strongest counterattack) simultaneously with the block, I mean that as soon as the opponent begins the attack, in your mind you have already counterattacked. In the second example of timing, when you block after the opponent's attack, unbalance the opponent by touching his arm, shoulder or other part to allow yourself extra time to counterattack.

As you make basic one time sparring remember that every time your opponent attacks, you have to find out where to step, what kind of counterattack to use, when you have to start to move and how far from your opponent you can stand. Concentrate your mind on the opponent's mind and catch the moment your opponent decides to come, then simultaneously block and counterattack as you move to a stronger position than before.

These are some points to check when you make basic ippon gumite. From beginning rei to ending rei, watch your opponent's eyes. Never look down or look away even when you finish an attack and are getting ready for the next one.

Some attackers are making a weak stance before they attack. After the oizuki, carefully check your stance, as many people either lose their balance, stand up high or stand on one leg.

Some people feel comfortable standing where their opponent can already hit them (inside the ma) and then stepping forward, taking a long time to prepare their mind and measure the distance. They have the idea that the opponent won't counterattack until they make an attack, so they feel very safe. They don't worry about anything until they are all ready. Then they attack. This is all wrong! You have to throw this attitude away. In ippon gumite you are practicing for a real situation. So when you face an opponent, feel that the opponent can come at any time to destroy you. Distance and timing have to be precise and exact, neither too close nor too far. Create just the right distance, watch your opponent's eyes and, during his weakest moment, get in. That is basic ippon gumite attack.

It is the same on the defending side. Most people very carelessly think, "Oh, an opponent never comes unless they step forward and make gedan barai. Then they just tell you when they start." Realistically, somebody jumps on you without warning. Therefore, you have to be ready for anything when you face somebody. Even before you bow, you have to feel that your opponent can really jump on you at any moment. You have to keep the right distance and be ready to move forward or backward or to the side.

Another bad habit is in the defender's movement to escape an attack. The problem comes when you start sideways, stepping with the left leg to the left and you try to block the opponent's attack with your left hand. When you do this, you become a larger target for your opponent's punch or kick. And when you move your left leg to the left, that's already one motion, so you have to make two motions to get out. When you are defending against a good opponent, you only have time for one movement which should place you in a stronger position than your opponent.

You can't make unreasonable, weak movements over and over when you practice sparring. Each movement has to be changed until you find the ideal movement, and every time you have to criticize yourself. Try many different ways of making blocks and counterattacks and then you will find your best techniques. Don't stick with a bad stance, bad movements or bad counterattacks and repeat these many times. Otherwise, these will become your habits, and then when you face a strong opponent, your techniques won't work.

Kihon Ippon Gumite from Hanmi (Half-facing Stance):

Originally, there was no basic ippon gumite from hanmi stance. However we should not let our basic form of karate practice blind us to the realistic situation, so this practice is a bridge between basic ippon gumite and a realistic fight. Both opponents show half-body to each other and practice executing various techniques: front leg, front arm, oizuki, gyakuzuki or rear leg kick. We are trying to make a situation closer to real combat, where both attacker and defender are in a position to attack or block. When both sides are ready to either attack or block, it changes the feeling of the match.

When we practice basic ippon gumite, we feel very comfortable about the attack because our opponent's centerline is open. If we have the habit of facing straight toward the opponent with our centerline open, it's not exactly realistic. In a real situation, we should not open our centerline to the opponent. When you are defending from hanmi stance, you can hide your centerline where you have many vital points. Also in a real case, an opponent doesn't always stands with his centerline open. When your opponent stands with hanmi, you should know how to attack or how to block his attack and be ready to make your counterattack.

For most of the Budo (martial arts) world, hanmi is the normal stance. Nobody stands with his two legs facing forward and all of his weak points exposed to the opponent. Hanmi is the basic stance, therefore see how your opponent sees you. Not only with your imagination, but how your opponent actually sees you. Practice in front of a mirror and remember what kind of posture you are giving to the opponent.

I suggest you practice in hanmi stance sometimes not only because it is very realistic, but also because it is the only stance where you can move in every direction when you face your opponent. When you face the opponent squarely, you can move to the side or back, but you cannot go forward with one motion. With hanmi, you can go left, right, back and also into the opponent. You should practice this with either leg forward until you are comfortable from both sides.

Beginners can make this practice, but instructors should know that most juniors are not ready to block well in this stance. They should also make basic ippon gumite from the ordinary stances.

Kihon Ippon Gumite from Kibadachi:

When we make ippon gumite with kibadachi, we can move as quickly as in other stances, but usually we cannot move with the open legs forward, because that's very dangerous. Therefore, we practice movements of kibadachi to the side. Or you can step with "S" movements, starting with the right or left leg front and then moving with the opposite leg into the opponent's centerline and making another kibadachi. That step is very useful for real combat.

We also make ippon gumite using kibadachi with the counterattack. This is to learn how to move in kibadachi against a real opponent. When the opponent comes with a right hand attack, you step back with the right leg, blocking the opponent's right hand attack with your right hand, your left hand counterattacking your opponent's right armpit. You have to control your counterattack exactly because you can damage your opponent's ribs easily. So, never touch in the counterattack. I hope everybody studies kime through this kibadachi and a front hand attack or rear hand gyakuzuki.

Kihon Ippon Gumite with Extra-Low Stances:

You have to make it a habit to keep your hips low in sparring, even though this basic training is hard and painful. Some schools like Shotokai, where Master Egami led, taught this extremely low stance, with hips at the level of the knees. The reason is that, in a real fight, everybody's feeling automatically goes up. And when we make contact with the opponent's body, the height of the hips is the key to keeping our balance, so we want our hips lower than our opponent's. Therefore, we have to always practice as low as possible and anticipate that we are going to come up a little bit in real time. Keeping low hips also brings our most courageous feeling from the bottom of our mind.

In real combat what's important isn't just physical movement, strength, technical excellence or refinement, but a strong mentality, facing the opponent with continuous energy, patience and the power of explosion. The low stances that we emphasize in Shotokan are a key to polishing and keeping a strong mentality. With a low stance, an extra strong mentality is required because we get tired easier and it is much more difficult to move. We must be very strict with ourselves or we cannot maintain our form. If we challenge ourselves to keep a low stance, it is a very effective training method. Remember that the hips should never be lower than the knees because the stance gets weaker and you'll injure your knees.

Kihon Ippon Gumite with Uraken:

Use uraken (back punch) when you attack. One practice is to step in and make uraken like an oizuki. Another practice is to slide in and make uraken.

There are three ways to use uraken as a counterattack. First, step back, hit the attack down and make uraken as a counterattack. Second, step in with both arms up, then hit down with uraken to the opponent's face or chest. Third make a mutual escape with both sides making uraken. With the last technique, neither side is trying to escape but if you both attack strongly with your best uraken at the same time, it will be like you pass through each other's attack. If one side hesitates, he will get hit.

Karate people in the world are not practicing back punch as much as before, but you shouldn't forget that uraken requires less effort to learn and is a very realistic, effective technique. Therefore, practice many uraken as a counterattack, making a small target, and making it exactly, hitting a vital point.

Kihon Ippon Gumite with Gyakuzuki as a Counterattack:

Sometimes you should practice basic ippon gumite using only gyakuzuki as your counterattack. No matter how you move to avoid the attack, you have to make a solid stance with strong hips when you execute the reverse punch. The back heel and the back leg must be connected with your hip movements and with the execution of the punch.

Kihon Ippon Gumite with Kicks as Attacks:

One of the best ways to learn to face real kicks is in basic one time sparring. We need to practice until we know that we can handle a kicking attack. In this practice it's easy to damage your hands, arm or wrist, or your opponent's toes and this damage can sometimes last a lifetime so always make your thumb tight, make a tight fist and don't get a kick in the fingers, because it's very easy to break your fingers. Don't hit your opponent's toes with your fist because you can break them. Be sure to tell your opponent which leg you are kicking with and also what target area. Then start with slow motion. This way many useless injuries can be avoided.

I know people a long time ago who were practicing kicks and blocking each other. One side broke his ankle and the other side broke his forearm. So, be very careful not to damage each other. As I always emphasize, if we want to be able to continue practicing together for many years, thousands of kicks and thousands of blocks, we have to be careful. If we get injured in the beginning, we cannot continue until we reach a good level. So you must keep your agreement and kick honestly, exactly, only that kick, only that certain level. Only speed and power change. Don't show off or humiliate anyone. When you kick, give your opponent a good chance to practice and then you can expect the same from him.

We practice five ways to defend against kicks:
- harai-uke (sweeping blocks)
- ma-o-kiru (cut the distance)
- lifting the knee
- nagewaza (throwing techniques against kicks)
- irimi (getting in)

Harai-uke means a sweeping block. Against kicks we usually use gedan barai (lower level sweeping blocks) both from the inside and the outside. We have to think how we can take advantage of the opponent when they kick. With a block we can destroy our opponent's leg and body as soon as he comes to attack. In a real case we can use gedan barai to crush the opponent's toes, ankles or shin as part of the counterattack. When you make gedan barai in the real case, you must execute it strongly and right after you block you must make a strong counterattack such as gyakuzuki. In practice don't hurt yourself or your opponent when you practice this blocking technique. It can still be very strong and throw the opponent off balance but be sure to use the block against a strong part of the leg such as the shin instead of a weak part such as the toes.

Ma-o-kiru means cutting the distance. You have to cut the distance between you and your opponent exactly, precisely. Remain just beyond the range of the kick when you step back. As the opponent's kick misses, shift your hips toward the opponent and execute a counterattack as his kicking leg touches the ground.

If there is no other way to step out or avoid the kick, just lift your knee and get the kick in your leg to protect your body. This is very effective but you have to sacrifice your leg to block your opponent's kick. Without raising the leg, you can simply step in before the opponent's kick is at its strongest and push the opponent back with your stomach. Taking the opponent's kick like this is effective but it will cost you a match in a tournament. Tournament rules have made some realistic movements like these disappear, but we should keep them for the real case.

We also practice throwing techniques against kicks. Position and timing are very important when you try to throw your opponent. Especially emphasize and apply the throw at the end of Heian Godan.

Irimi is getting into the opponent. This is kind of risky until you learn that the human mind can be strong and positive. At the moment the opponent decides to destroy you, you get in. Your courageous mind can turn away your cowardice and self-concern and you can go into your opponent to escape the kick.

Kihon Ippon Gumite with Kicks as Counterattacks:
One of the special techniques of karate, compared with any other martial arts, is our kicks. When you practice counterattacks with kicks, no

matter how the opponent comes, your legs have to be free to kick powerfully.

The strongest part of any kick is the standing leg. Any time you execute a kick, you have to consider that you are supporting not only the weight of your whole body, but also your opponent's momentum, weight and focus, all with the standing leg. Therefore, when you move to the side or back, the standing leg has to be strong. Small people, especially, have to make an exact target and attack the opponent's weakest points with the kick.

We sometimes execute kicks as a counter in ippon gumite a little late. But if your kicks are even a little late, they will never work. So when you want to use kicks, you have to find out the opponent's starting moment and kick quickly enough.

Kihon Ippon Gumite using Counterattacks with Rotating Hips:

In kumite, we are not always stepping forward or backward on the line. Sometimes we rotate our hips when blocking or evading the opponent's attack, and then simultaneously we can execute one of the most powerful counterattacks: swinging punch, uraken or mawashigeri. If one of these is your favorite technique, be sure to practice rotating hips when you block or evade and make a strong, simultaneous counterattack.

Kihon Ippon Gumite with Upper Level Attacks:

We originally practiced the same amount of upper level attacks as middle level attacks. But we have to avoid accidents and injuries, so we practice more middle level attacks. Still, we have to know how to defend against upper level attacks, and how to attack upper level.

Upper level means from under the nose to the throat. Don't attack above eye level. The attacker's fist is a little above shoulder height so you can attack the center of the opponent's chin, or a little bit higher or lower.

You have to execute a straight attack exactly to the opponent's chin when you practice. The purpose is not to hurt your opponent, but to attack seriously. You must avoid unrealistic practice, because then our practice becomes meaningless. For example, when you make an upper level attack, you don't punch away from the opponent's face. You have to feel you are really penetrating the opponent's face, the punch going straight to the

Kumite 169

opponent's upper level. Then we can practice together and really improve our sparring.

On the blocking side, you've go to feel when your opponent first decides to come attack. At this moment you can block strongly and you don't have to worry about getting punched in the face. Of course, when you are a beginner, you have mental blocks about somebody coming to punch your face and you try to avoid the punch by turning your head or blinking momentarily. But this blind moment in front of the opponent's fist is very dangerous.

Even though the attacker is coming straight to the upper level, your feeling should be the same as when the attacker is coming to stomach level. You have to tighten your mind and watch the opponent's eyes and have confidence that you can see the opponent's attack clearly. You have to know that an opponent's upper level attack is weaker than a middle level attack because your opponent's feeling comes up and the fist separates from the rest of the body. It's actually very easy to move the opponent's fist. It's not like when the opponent comes with low hips to the middle level with the fist and underarm connected.

I'll give you one more hint: if you try to block far from your face, with your arm extended to the opponent's powerful shoulder and upper arm, it's very difficult. But, if you block close to your face, the opponent's arm is extended. That makes his arm weaker and your blocking arm is much more powerful.

Everybody has mental blocks in the beginning, but with many repetitions of this practice you get the habit of watching the opponent's start and learn how you can get out from an upper level attack.

Kihon Ippon Gumite with a Double Attack:

Traditionally there is no two-time engagement match. Realistically, people attack with two attacks, not just one. As you know, one of the boxers' specialties is the one-two punch. So have your opponent attack with two punches, for example: one to the face, the other to the stomach; one to the eyes, the second to the nose. Utilize more of a sliding step on the attack, perhaps both attacks with just one step. Defending side must figure out how to block to get out. If you practice much sanbon gumite without blocks, this will help you immensely. Otherwise you will have trouble figuring out what to do.

Jiyu Kumite (Free Sparring)

In jiyu kumite (free sparring) either side can attack at any time after the command to start, with any technique. All techniques are controlled.

Jiyu means free, not only with our techniques, but also with our mentality. The mind has to be free from any kind of restriction. Jiyu kumite lets us work on a calm, controlled mentality with strategic movements as a practice for real fights. But don't think that this is the closest to real combat. Jiyu ippon gumite is much closer.

Many people consider only the mechanics of jiyu kumite, such as timing and distance but the main thing is actually your mentality. What kind of feeling do you have? Your mentality must be alert to see your opponent's feeling and your feeling, too.

Two things are especially important in improving your mentality. The first is that you must penetrate your fear. In the beginning it is normal to be uncomfortable or afraid but you can get through that by deciding not to turn your head away or close your eyes when your opponent attacks. You have to decide to face each opponent straight — never turn around — and then make your strongest gyakuzuki or other counterattack each time your opponent attacks. The second point is that you must have a favorite technique you feel confidence in. You have to practice your favorite technique many thousands of times until you feel you can depend on this technique in any situation, no matter what kind of opponent you are facing. After you learn to face each opponent without turning away and have an effective favorite technique, then I think it takes about 500 serious experiences in jiyu kumite to reach the point where you feel no fear about sparring.

To make so many matches takes a long time and every time we practice jiyu kumite, there are many risks. When you're young, you don't mind getting little injuries, but without complete control, you cannot continue your practice over many years. This is because even a small injury sometimes becomes a very serious health problem. So we have to be very careful in our practice to avoid accidents and serious injuries that could cause permanent damage.

We have to control our attacks completely, stopping just in front of the opponent's skin. Many people consciously try to stop, but unconsciously they have a weak feeling and hurt other people. The body is very honest, so even in our unconscious we shouldn't have a bit of immature feeling. We must be very strict with ourselves and practice complete control of all our techniques. Even if our opponent hits us by mistake, we should not get upset and retaliate. When a person reaches this mental level, he understands the ideal practice of jiyu kumite.

Of course, at the same time we are avoiding accidents, we also have to have a realistic feeling. Jiyu kumite is used in tournaments as a game and this has led to some problems. Recent tournament fighters are quite good at that game, but from a realistic viewpoint many of them have lost the kime (focus to make an effective technique) and the real fighting mentality. We have to remember that there is a difference between a tournament and a real fight. We are practicing for real, so we always criticize ourselves and find out for ourselves what works and what doesn't. We look for techniques which destroy the opponent, not ones that just touch his skin.

Practicing together, we are seeking the basic elements, the basic understanding which ancient people left to us, and are trying to digest it. There are many elements which we cannot describe by words that can only be experienced in serious practice. Through our practice each of us can find our unique strength and feeling. This is what we are seeking as martial artists.

Slow Jiyu Kumite:

We have to apply all of our practice in realistic combat, and so between our practice and real combat we have to make many jiyu kumite matches. One of the methods we use to avoid accidents and to learn more about the connection between us and our opponents is to make very slow jiyu kumite.

In addition to being less dangerous, practicing jiyu kumite in slow motion gives us much better opportunities to find our blind spots, places where we leave ourselves open for attack and weak moments in our mentality. When we are practicing in slow motion, we look for our own weaknesses. Also, when we make slow motion jiyu kumite, most people have great difficulty pushing their hips into the opponent. Even when practicing in slow motion, you should try to move into the opponent with strong, low hips, positioning yourself so that the angle of the opponent's stance becomes weaker. This lets you see whether your stance is really effective or not.

In slow jiyu kumite a mature person goes slower, while an immature person increases the speed. The mature feeling is always on the slower side. When you shift gears to quicker movements unconsciously, you have to see yourself as the side with the weaker mentality. This is a race to see who is more mature, and slower is better. The idea is not to see if you can touch your opponent with a quick attack or protect yourself with a quick block. Instead, we are looking for the connection between ourselves and our opponent. We want to see how something we do changes the opponent's mind or body. Slow jiyu kumite lets us experience this connection which is hard to experience other ways.

You also have to practice normal speed, which is real combat practice, but slow and quick are relative. There is no such thing as "quicker is better."

Jiyu Kumite and Close Combat:

Close combat is our worst ability, especially when we compare ourselves to other martial artists in sumo or judo or even aikido. These people fight from a much closer distance than we do. To face this kind of opponent we should study techniques we can use from a close distance.

If somebody is very quick and gets too close to you, the first point is don't get upset, choke up or just step back. Accept the narrow distance and calm down, with no conscious power in your shoulders. Keep your elbows in, cover your weak points and never show your centerline to your opponent.

Next look at effective techniques. As a start, practice chudan or jodan udeuke with a partner, very close. Touching the inside of each other's wrists, hook each other. From there, one side starts to attack carefully and then blocks carefully. We can learn how to move our bodies and how to make an effective counterattack. Learn how to make a strong stance and execute your techniques without losing your balance. Then we can develop close combat techniques such as elbow attacks and kneeing techniques. These are very difficult to control, so be careful not to hit the opponent. Usually one side attacks and then the other side attacks. Don't attack simultaneously until you really get used to this practice. You can also work on uraken, reverse punch and throwing techniques, especially from kibadachi. But don't forget, if you try to use throwing techniques against judo experts, they can throw you very easily.

Even worse than close combat is when you are actually thrown. This is called newaza, wrestling on a mat. In this situation, judo people can take you very easily by choking you and locking your elbows, legs or neck. Still, we have one second to make our strongest counterattack, to make the opponent weaker or cause him to momentarily lose consciousness. So, learning how to make a powerful counterattack in case your are on the ground with the opponent is our goal in newaza practice. If you miss the moment, you won't have a chance. Use your fist, fingers, elbows, knees, toes or heels, anything you can, to make your strongest attack as soon as you are on the ground and the opponent is on top of you.

Close combat is one of the blind spots of the karate practitioners, who have the longest distance of the weaponless martial arts. We are careless about how we stand until we bow to each other. Some other people don't care about the martial arts. They don't bow in the beginning. They don't keep what we think is a proper distance. They just suddenly jump on us. Martial artists should be ready for this. We should get out from mental blocks that we always have a flat floor or that we always have to bow or that there's a referee and a certain distance when we start. There is no such rule. There is only one rule in martial arts, and that is no rule. So to be a real martial artist, close combat is one of the practices we need to understand.

Practicing Control in Jiyu Kumite:
You don't have any right in jiyu kumite to make contact with your opponent. Therefore, before you practice jiyu kumite, you must practice control. We practice with one side standing in natural stance while the other side jumps in and attacks upper level and middle level, making two or three continuous attacks with complete control.

If you do this practice several times, you realize that control depends on your own mental strength. If you decide strongly, "I never touch," you don't touch. If you don't do this and just make excuses, "Oh, I was going to control, but my fist went or my leg went," you are only fooling yourself and nobody has to believe you.

You consider your life important — the most precious thing is your life — so consider other people's lives, too. Don't make hitting somebody the purpose of your practice and don't hit anybody because you can't control yourself. This is very immature.

Long Distance Jiyu Kumite:

Long distance jiyu kumite is a duel fought starting from a long distance, especially when done outside. When you are facing an opponent in a real situation, you don't expect the opponent to come closer, salute and then start. If the opponent doesn't do that, what are you going to do? You cannot complain about his bad manners.

No matter what kind of opponent, no matter what place, inside or outside, start the engagement from a far distance. Make your feeling penetrate your opponent. Every inch, every step, you have to measure. You have to feel. You can read his strategy, discover his favorite techniques, his rhythm and condition. You have to see your opponent's weak points, weak moments and execute your strongest attack to destroy him. From the farthest distance you have to concentrate on going through and destroying your opponent.

This practice is part of the examination for fourth dan in Shotokan.

Jiyu Ippon Gumite (Free One Time Sparring)

Jiyu ippon gumite is one real attack to a specified target followed by a controlled counterattack from the defender. In this practice the attacker may move freely to create an opening for the specified attack.

Jiyu ippon gumite is the most characteristic practice method of Shotokan and we believe that this is the closest practice to real combat. This is where we face an opponent knowing that every time he is going to make his best attack to try to destroy us. From this we learn to read the opponent's mind, find out best sense of ma (distance and timing), find the best strategy and the most effective attack and block and counterattack.

Like babies learn hot and cold for themselves, we have to learn these important aspects of sparring for ourselves by practicing jiyu ippon gumite many times. We cannot learn with our conscious, intellectual mind. We have to train with a strong mentality and repeat this practice until we understand it.

In jiyu ippon gumite, after the salute, right away both sides must be ready. No matter what kind of sudden attack or tricky attack your opponent makes, you are ready to make a counterattack. If, in your mind, you are negative and feel like you don't want to get a punch or you want to get out from your opponent's attack, you lose the chance to make an effective counterattack. Therefore, in your mind, only concentrate on how to make the most effective counterattack the moment the opponent decides to come attack.

As the attacker, you attack a particular level, a particular point, with a particular side and technique. You cannot switch sides and attack with either right or left, or change the attacking technique. Our basic understanding is that, if you start punching with the right hand, you continue with that hand. If you are making oizuki, don't attack with gyakuzuki. And, if you are attacking a particular level, middle level for instance, attack the solar plexus. Middle level is not shoulder level or belt level; it is exactly stomach level.

Of course, if both agree, you can alternate, first attacking with your right hand, the next attack with your left and so on. Or you can say today we are going to practice only oizuki with the left hand to middle level. You've got to make it clear before you start, exactly what the rule will be. Then the attacker can go with full strength.

When you attack, you have to be realistic and make your attack with one motion and get in with full strength and speed. Watch your opponent's eyes. Don't try to trick the opponent while inside ma (the distance where the opponent can get you). Of course, you can switch the direction, switch the timing outside the ma, that's your choice. And you don't have to make a straight line. You can make a different course. And you can make any strategic or psychological change to confuse and disturb your opponent's concentration. But when you attack, go straight to the opponent's centerline with your strongest energy and focus. Don't attack in any other direction. Then turn quickly. The more experienced opponents are, the more distance they can execute the exchange from. After more experience, you can practice jumping in with the attack. Each time you have to ask yourself if this is realistic. Can I do this or not?

After the defending side makes an effective counterattack, he can attack right away so don't feel comfortable after your opponent's counterattack. Right after you make a really solid counterattack, keeping a continuous relationship with your opponent's mind, you can charge him as the attacker. Some people misunderstand and because they want to damage their opponent or show they are superior to him, they eliminate a solid counterattack and only think about the next attack. This is the wrong feeling; you must make an effective counterattack first.

On the other hand, some people make a weak attack so they never give their opponent a chance to make a counterattack. They make it like jiyu kumite. In jiyu ippon gumite you must make a complete attack.

There are several other points you need to keep in mind to make a realistic jiyu ippon gumite practice.

The rule for jiyu ippon gumite is that the defender makes an effective, controlled counterattack as the attacker is making a real attack. Some people misunderstand and think that, as the attacker, if they step into the ma and wait for the opponent to move they have the right to punch before the opponent is allowed to make his counterattack. This is not true. First of all you don't have the right to smash somebody's face while he waits and does nothing. Secondly, it's not realistic. In a real fight the opponent doesn't have to wait until you punch him before he counterattacks, and in a real fight the counterattack is not controlled. If you get too close to your opponent, you have made your attack whether you actually throw a punch or not. If you're holding back your punch inside ma, a good opponent will have already beaten you. You have to remember that this is a practice for a real situation and not make any artificial rules about the timing of the engagement.

It is important to not always initiate an attack or counterattack the way that the opponent is expecting. Don't always employ the same routine. Think strategically. Vary the timing, position and focus, without losing a strong feeling. Look for the weak moment in your opponent's mind and get in at precisely that moment.

When we are attacking stomach level, and you know the opponent will attack stomach level, don't hide the stomach. This is not realistic at all. Why would an opponent come to attack stomach level if you are not open there? You have to be open there, so they have a chance to punch your stomach. From there you have to block or evade or irimi or anything and make a strong counterattack. The same thing is true for upper level. If your opponent is attacking upper level, don't cover your face from the beginning. That is the wrong attitude.

When you are the attacker, you want to get closer, but when you block, you want to keep a longer distance from the opponent. That is wrong. That's showing your level is lower than your opponent's, or that your mentality is not as clear as your opponent's. You have to sense the ma (distance and timing) between you and your opponent. In the realistic case, there is no difference between the ma when you are attacking and the ma when the opponent is attacking. There is only one ma. You may have an extremely powerful attack, well connected, with good focus, but without a sense of ma it is wasted. You will never be able to really face an opponent. Ma is that important. You can almost say if someone understands ma, they *are* the winner.

As soon as the opponent decides to attack you, make your strongest counterattack. The key to the counterattack is to make the strongest counterattack you can and still have perfect control. In the practice, none of us has the right to injure the opponent. We have a saying, if you hurt your body, that damage can last your whole life. So you concentrate, you give your strongest feeling and most serious attitude and attack with your full strength, but control completely. These are two contradictory elements, but everyone who practices karate has to understand them.

Originally I translated this practice as one attack engagement, but somebody made it one attack, semi-free style. I don't remember who translated it this way but semi-free style for jiyu ippon gumite gives the impression that jiyu ippon gumite is a little bit inferior to jiyu kumite. The general public may get the impression that jiyu kumite is a more advanced, more realistic or more difficult type of kumite. My respected senior, Master Shuntaro Ito from Keio University, one of Master Funakoshi's top pupils, was always telling us that jiyu ippon gumite is the most realistic kumite practice. With it you can really compare who is superior without any accidents. I completely agree with Master Ito's viewpoint. One reason is that jiyu kumite is physically and mentally, completely controlled. With jiyu ippon gumite, when you attack with a real attack, you can feel you're really getting into the opponent.

Jiyu ippon gumite is the meeting point of all different types of karate schools. It shows who the strong, realistic fighters are. This practice shows the real strength in real combat, without any accidents or injuries, humiliation or mental stress, so you can see the real level. Already your opponent knows you're coming with the right fist to his face, so you can go as realistically as possible, with your strongest attack. Somebody who cannot make a counterattack, doesn't have a chance to face this person in real combat. If you don't have any trouble to make your strongest counterattack, completely controlled, you can face this man in a real fight.

Jiyu ippon gumite is the most realistic form of kumite and we can use this feeling in real combat. This is the top method of fighting practice. The only higher level is a real duel.

Jiyu Ippon Gumite with Ashibarai (Sweeps) and Nagewaza (Throws):

Emphasize applying throwing techniques as part of your counterattack. Keep your hips close to your opponent's and also lower than his. Throwing itself is not enough. Every time when you throw, immediately you have to execute a kick or punch and make sure you completely destroy the opponent. Never stop after just a throw and go on to the next opponent because your opponent may not be hurt by your throw and can come back and attack you again.

Being able to do the ashibarai to an opponent is not enough. You have to practice what to do when the opponent comes to sweep you, too.

Jiyu Ippon Gumite with Tobikomi (Jumping In) Attacks:

This is a practice for you to show your strong spirit as well as your physical powers. For this practice when you make tobikomi, you have to jump in to the opponent from outside the ma with one feeling and make kime (a completely focused attack). This is part of being a realistic combat fighter.

Any jumping in attack creates a moment when the opponent feels a little weak and cannot react or else he has to step back. This mentality suggests a negative feeling or, strategically, a desire not to come in. When the opponent starts to step back, jump in deeper than he expects. To do this you must decide very strongly, with your mind penetrating far behind your opponent's head.

On the other hand, when you are defending and the opponent comes with a vigorous, positive feeling and a powerful attack, don't inhale, shrink or rise higher. Instead lower your hips and turn to the opponent's blind side, making the opponent lose his target and giving you the best counterattack. This jiyu ippon gumite with tobikomi oizuki was the favorite practice at Waseda University when I was a student there.

When making this kumite with jumping-in kicks, the blocking side must step back very far or step into the opponent, without losing the best moment to execute the counterattack.

Jiyu Ippon Gumite with Uraken (Back Fist):

We practice jiyu-ippon gumite with uraken both as an attack and as a counterattack. As an attack, first practice making uraken stepping in with the rear foot, like oizuki. Then, with yoriashi, make uraken with the front hand, like maete. As a counter, make the block and uraken as one continuous movement. Or, you don't even have to block and can make uraken directly as a counterattack. Any way you make uraken, if you go with your hips and no conscious power in the shoulder and arms and swing very smoothly, and at the last minute, when you touch the opponent's vital points, connect with the hip's motion, it's effective.

There are five ways we use uraken as a counterattack: (1) step in with a right or left arm uraken, (2) slide in with uraken from a front stance or kibadachi, (3) step back and block with tetsui and then make uraken, (4) step in, raise both arms, the back arm blocks up and the front arm counters down with uraken, (5) practice a mutual penetration with your opponent. Both opponents step in at the same time with uraken attacking to the temple. If you feel the same as your opponent, neither of you will get hit.

Jiyu Ippon Gumite with Kicks:

While making kumite with kicks, many people hurt their thumb or fingers when they block the opponent's kick because they open their fist. However, when you make a tight fist and block strongly, you can break the opponent's toes or shin. Therefore, when you practice jiyu ippon gumite using kicks, be careful. Don't injure your thumb or fingers or your opponent's toes.

You should try to make your opponent feel uncomfortable. Sometimes we have a blind spot to the sides for catching kicks. Try to pick it up from watching your opponent's eyes, not by watching his legs.

Jiyu Ippon Gumite with Maete (Jab):

When an opponent comes with a strong maete to your face, what are you going to do? Most people block with the front hand, but it is a better idea to use the rear hand to block. Once you can make jiyu ippon gumite with maete, then learn to counterattack with maete also.

Self Defense

The Japanese term for self-defense is goshin-jutsu. "Go" means protect, "shin" means our own being or body and "jutsu" means technique.

We are not interested in street fights and ask all of our members to avoid stupid fights with people who have low mentalities. We do not have time or energy to waste our life on things like that. On the other hand, if someone jumps on you in the dark without any reason, you have to defend yourself. I don't like to hear that someone who has become a black belt in Shotokan still doesn't have any ability to handle situations in the street.

Pretend some guy comes with any attack, to see if you can apply your techniques. Find out if you can defend yourself. If you react okay, that's fine, but if you react stupidly, you have to criticize your stupidity or blind points in your practice and fix them. We should never forget that karate is based on real combat. We should be able to apply our traditional karate practice to any situation. Don't make any excuse for your own practice, especially when you are practicing basics and katas. You always have to keep in mind that these techniques are for real combat.

We study realistic fighting as a separate practice because ordinary people in the streets don't attack like a karate attack with a straight oizuki. Most of the time they attack with a swinging motion which is much easier to see and block. All karate practitioners can block an opponent's oizuki, but some of us don't know what to do when someone comes with a swinging attack. Therefore, sometimes we practice for opponents like drunks or crazy guys who jump us on the street and attack with swinging fists and one-two punches.

These practices should stick with simple, realistic and effective techniques and repeat them until they can be applied in a real situation. Self-defense practice is not just mechanical motions. In order to master one self-defense technique so that it can be applied to many different situations, we have to practice this same motion many thousands of times. Don't make fancy, complicated techniques. Udeuke-fumikomi (forearm block and stamping) is the most realistic basic practice for self-defense, especially if you are a small person facing a larger opponent.

When you practice other techniques, always use your imagination to find out how you can escape from the opponent's attack, and what kind of realistic counterattack you can make. Don't just follow the opponent's one-two punch, but see if you can apply your understanding of getting into the opponent as he starts to attack. Always, we have to think. There is no limit, and no particular technique. Keep your knowledge of how to apply basics but apply it without rules to make your counterattacks with your full strength exactly on one of your opponent's vital points. Everybody use your imagination and find your own favorite, realistic techniques.

We have to remember that, no matter what movements or techniques, the most important element in real combat is mental strength. So what we are practicing through many daily practices and special trainings is our mentality, how we can face difficulties any time, any place, with any opponent.

Please don't misunderstand, I'm not encouraging you to get in trouble in the street. The best in best never gets into trouble and never has to use these techniques. Basically we're prohibited from using our karate techniques against ordinary people in a street fight. You never have the right to hit somebody first. Even if you think you have a reason, you don't have to get into a fight.

That's why we are practicing. We don't have to get upset and go crazy and damage other people. The best martial artist never gets involved in real combat or fights in a street fight in his whole life.

Continuous Attack

After Shodan, people usually begin practicing continuous attacks. The main point is not the physical movements, but the mental attitude. When we decide to destroy the opponent, we must have a strong, continuous feeling of power going through our opponent. We can't change our mind. We can't cut our breathing. We can't even blink. We just have to continue to go through until the end. If you understand this mentality, then all techniques will follow this feeling.

Your mental preparation and penetration begin before you face your opponent. Your mentality penetrates the opponent with strong, continuous energy. You have already decided very strongly not to stop until you destroy your opponent. When you decide to get into your opponent, you don't stop after one technique. Instead you continue with one, two, three, four attacks until the opponent falls to the ground. The point is not continuous physical movement or repetition of mechanical techniques, but your strong mentality penetrating the opponent. Breathing and mentality should be continuous until the opponent falls.

It may sound cruel or vicious or crazy, but what you learn is that once your mind is completely free from fear and worry about yourself, the only important thing left is destroying your opponent. If you have this mentality, your body will always follow continuously. It's not just punching once and waiting for your opponent to fall down. It's one punch or kick and then right away another punch or kick and another and another, continuously, until the opponent goes down.

One viewpoint is that against bigger, heavier or much tougher opponents, if the opponent is not destroyed, even when you attack with very good kime (focused power), then you must attack continuously until he is completely destroyed. So don't make light, ineffective techniques because, no matter how many times you attack without kime, a tough opponent will always find a way to destroy you. You must feel that even your first attack will destroy the opponent completely, then continuously make more attacks. Each one has to be effective. This continuous, penetrating feeling brings out your favorite combination techniques.

Another viewpoint is that in real combat most people use less than 50 percent of their ability because they are excited or scared. Practice itself encourages us to increase our ability to express our best and, if somebody practices seriously and can truly bring all the strength he shows in practice into real combat, then he's already graduated to an expert's level. Somebody who can express their best, any time, against any opponent, is a master. Until that time, even if we can express ourselves 100 percent in practice, we can only express 50 percent or less in a real situation. Therefore, we have to make it up with something else. So we practice combinations and continuous attacks and, although we do not want to have to depend on a second or third attack, it's much wiser to practice this way. Of course, in a practice we cannot hurt our opponents, and we have to tell ourselves, "This is practice." But in a real situation, there is no limit and no stopping.

One practice we make is continuous attack with maete, maegeri and gyakuzuki. Defender can only block stepping back or stepping to the side. This is not exactly realistic, but the practice has to be this way so that the attacker can practice freely. If the defender does not step back and there is a crash, the risk of injury is very high. The attacker should have a realistic, strong feeling, but avoid needless accidents. In a real case you can do anything — you can step in, you can destroy your opponent as soon as he starts to come.

On the defending side, we work on blocks, evading and irimi against continuous attacks. The opponent wants to kill you, and you not only try to get out, but get into the opponent as well. This is usually practiced with a continuous chudan-level oizuki attack. Some schools make this practice without stopping for 30 or 40 minutes, until both people are exhausted, falling on the floor and getting up again to continue. The main theme of the practice is the continuous feeling of the attacker and the blocker not having a passive feeling, but actually having a mentality stronger than the attacker's.

This is an extension of the "Gate of Heaven" practice we make as brown belts. When the opponent decides to come, you continuously give your whole face and body to the opponent's fist. You are not just waiting there for the attack. Your feeling must be much more positive, more aggressive. Then you can get out and evade.

We practice many times evading without blocks, but you also need to practice using your blocks to destroy the opponent. You don't hurt your practice partner, but be conscious of making strong blocks. When you are practicing blocks against continuous kicks, be careful not to allow your wrist or fingers to be weak. It is very easy to break your fingers.

Sometimes we make this practice in slow motion because at first everybody tries to make the body move with a weak mind and it doesn't work. With slow motion techniques you can feel like you have enough time to move strongly. However, slow motion has its own problems. It's very easy to fool yourself and increase the speed a little bit more than the opponent so you can hit or block them. Going faster is not realistic in this practice. The realistic way to make this practice is with moves slower than your opponent.

Slow or fast, it is very important to always keep a strong feeling. There should be no difference between practice and a real case. Always give your opponent your best feeling. This way you will help each other improve. One moment, when you really have a strong feeling, then, without thinking, your body starts to move and you ask yourself, "How come I could get out?" Because your mind is waking up, that's why. That's the feeling we are looking for when we practice continuous attacks.

Pushing Practice

When we get close, right away the opponent's weight and strength come onto our body and our techniques start to lose effectiveness. In basic pushing exercises we learn how to avoid an opponent's direct pushing power, and also how to use our whole body as one.

In all martial arts, we learn that when we contact each other's bodies, we have to express our strongest energy totally into the opponent's body. We cannot waste any power, especially a small person against a heavy opponent. We always keep our elbows in, with strong underarms and low hips and a strong stance. Then we get into the opponent and make the opponent's underarm weaker, make his elbow go out and make sure to push from a lower position to a higher position.

Sometimes you can make a ring and try to push your opponent out of the ring as they do in sumo. Other times you can push each other in a straight line across the dojo floor. Either way these exercises teach us important elements of combat.

It's quite difficult to push each other, especially when there is a big difference in size, but choose a partner the same size and try to push each other. When you're young, when you have lots of power, you can push each other a lot.

Torite (Escaping Techniques)

Torite are escaping techniques used against an opponent who is grabbing some part of your body. Torite originally referred to Japanese policemen because they would arrest and restrain people. There are two meanings for torite: one is to escape and the other is to hold. They are two different characters. Some people refer to it as take or arrest.

With torite, we think about a real situation. When an attacker comes to grab you, what are you going to do? How are you going to escape from a powerful opponent? You have to avoid a complete holding technique, never panic and remember that you always have a chance to escape from an opponent who is holding you.

Torite's most important essence and practice is for mental preparation. If someone gets too upset or emotional, it will take away from his mental and technical effectiveness. You must be very cool and calm, and have a strong feeling inside. Then you can apply your technique.

Everyone should work on learning techniques for escaping from a one-hand grab. Two-hand grabs or somebody coming from behind are for later on. In the beginning just work on the simple ones and repeat the basic movements until you can do them easily — only a few techniques practiced over and over.

The simple, one-hand techniques are designed to teach a small person how to escape from the grasp of a bigger, more powerful person. But please don't forget the special feature of karate, our kick and punch, before you try to escape. For instance, when someone grabs one of your arms, this is a great chance to execute your thrusting attack to the opponent's face with your free hand. When an opponent is holding you, your thrusting attack or kick is much more effective. If the opponent is free to move to the front or back, it is very hard to make an effective attack. When the opponent is holding you, it's very easy to destroy him.

So if you are not sure that you can get out with just your escaping technique, first kick the opponent's shin or groin, or attack the opponent's eyes or some other vital point. (You should practice making three techniques within one second; this is very effective.) Especially, practice fumikomi because it is the most effective technique for everyone when escaping. Even a small girl can break a hold by stamping on the instep or knee. Then you can use these torite techniques to effectively get out.

Sometime you may need to use these techniques in a real situation. In your mental preparation to escape, you must first try to prevent any conflict. If you can't, then you must be very careful and humble. In your mind, it is as if you have already escaped. The only way to extinguish the feeling of panic is to imagine situations every day and figure out how you would escape from them. You must also diligently practice the torite techniques.

The only difference between torite and our ordinary practice is that in torite someone is usually holding your hand or some part of your body. When somebody is touching you, no matter how you try to hide it, he can feel right away when you start to move and it's easy for him to stop you. Therefore, make one motion in the opposite direction from what you're going to do. In other words, we always make two motions for one escape. We call that tsukuri, which means fix. As in judo, when you want to throw to the left, you first pull to the right. When your opponent resists, at this moment you throw to the left.

As you progress to more difficult forms of torite, you will discover that torite is not just form; torite is also rhythm, timing and mentality. When making torite from sitting form, this sitting form itself leads us to ideal hip movements, so we should sit comfortably and make very free hip movements. Sometimes this feels uncomfortable. Until you feel comfortable when you sit, keep practicing. Only a few hundred repetitions is not good enough. You must repeat these techniques at least a thousand times.

When you are practicing torite as the attacker by holding your opponent's wrist or both arms or holding him from behind or from the side, try to be as realistic as possible. Don't make it too easy or too hard for your partner because you know what he is going to do. To be realistic means you don't expect anything. You just hold on to your opponent and let him practice how to get out. The first element is mechanical, the second is timing and the third is emptiness and fullness. When two people start to understand this, there is a rhythm between them.

One important part of this study is to know our strongest and weakest points compared to other martial arts. Our best distance is when we can almost touch the opponent with our hand, but not close enough to be grabbed. Keep that distance and you will be able to take advantage of someone trained in wrestling, sumo, judo or aikido. If you get closer and the opponent grabs you, remember they are experts in their own art, so respect their strength. Don't underestimate a well-trained judo-ka or aikido-ka. If they grab you, you cannot do anything. Therefore study how these experts are able to hold you and how you can use your techniques to keep a safe distance. Also, for the worst case, study what you can do if you are grabbed.

Kata-Te-Dori:

We call the escapes shown below the seven ways of kata-te-dori, or escaping from one-hand holds. Of course, nobody holds you with one hand like that. These very fundamental training methods are not intended to be realistic situations. A real case is much different from this kata-te-dori practice.

One Hand Grabs (Left Hand to Right Hand):

We practice the following escapes as part of our basic understanding. When you practice these escapes, be sure to practice against a grab to your left hand, too. Usually we practice five escaping techniques, all with the opponent's left hand holding your right wrist:

1. Your elbow goes to your opponent's elbow as your hips turn counterclockwise, your right hip going to the opponent's left hip. At the same time bend your wrist, escape the opponent's grabbing hand and attack the opponent's ribs with your left elbow or make uraken to the face.

2. Push your open hand between your opponent's legs, turning your wrist counterclockwise, and simultaneously turning your hips counterclockwise to the opponent's left hip and attack with the left elbow. This time your breathing goes into your fingers.

3. Exactly like Heian Sandan, movement 9, your hips go to the right wrist and then you twist your wrist to touch your hip and turn counterclockwise and step to the opponent's outside into kibadachi. Your wrist goes behind your back. Keep low hips when you turn and execute enpi (elbow attack) to the opponent's elbow or ribs. Don't escape with the power of the arm. Completely take conscious

power off from the wrist, shoulder and arm. Use your hip movements and you can get out.

4. This technique is from Kwanku, movement 55. Bend your elbow ninety degrees, hand up. Hold your opponent's arm at shoulder height, turn your small finger in and turn your hips counterclockwise and make uraken. You can grab the opponent's wrist to throw him if you want or just attack with uraken.

5. From Heian Shodan, movement 4, without any movements, but in your mind connecting your wrist and front hip, pull your wrist with your hips and make a big circle with your arm and with your breathing break your opponent's grasp. This is the most difficult torite to learn. I don't expect everybody to be able to do it very well, even though it seems very simple.

One Hand Grabs (Right Hand to Right Hand):

In another set of escapes the opponent's right hand grabs your right wrist from the inside. When you practice these escapes, be sure to practice against a grab to your left hand, too.

1. Bring your fist up 90 degrees. Step back with left leg, turn your wrist up, make a fist with one knuckle sticking out and attack the opponent's wrist from the inside with this fist (ippon-ken). Move your hips down and back, pull and unbalance your opponent. Take your arm away and execute an uraken (back fist attack) to your opponent's face.

2. Move your right leg to the rear and, with an open hand, move the wrist up to 90 degrees, with the shoulders and elbows down. Pull the opponent's arm, with the left palm going to the opponent's arm and locking his elbow. Then you can control your opponent.

Irimi (Getting into the Opponent)

"Iri" means to get in, "mi" is body. So irimi is getting into the opponent's body. Actually, it's not the body. It's really the opponent's mind that you get into when you make irimi.

Irimi means that at the moment when the opponent decides to move, just as the decision comes into the opponent's mind, you decide to move, too. The essence of irimi is very difficult to explain in words. You can't understand it with theories or by using your conscious mind, but you can experience it. Real understanding comes only through your experience. There is a saying, "Under the sword is hell; through the sword is heaven." Irimi is how you get through the sword.

Irimi is joining with the opponent's aggressive mentality. This is not some movement or technique. If you don't have a strong mentality or are concerned for yourself, your movements cannot be irimi. Irimi is to get *into* the opponent — literally getting into the opponent's mind and body. If there is even the slightest idea that you want to get out from or avoid the opponent's attack, already there is no sense of irimi.

Brown belts who go to special training all know about the starting practice of irimi. We call it "Gate of Heaven" (in Japanese this is Ten No Mon). To practice, the attacking side comes with an ideal oizuki, trying to penetrate your mind and body. With your strong mentality, you face this opponent's strongest attack. Still, your mind goes into the opponent and you are not trying to avoid the opponent's strong attack. Don't worry about yourself. The moment the opponent comes to destroy you, you just throw away your ego and get into the opponent's body.

Real irimi is even more. You don't really exist. Your mind is beyond just penetrating your opponent's mind because it has already happened. Irimi is a state of mind. Your mind, body and fist become completely one. When somebody reaches the mature, strong, clean mentality and overcomes his fear of the opponent's physical strength, then he can apply this feeling in real combat.

Anyone with a courageous mind and a mentality that is not concerned with self can break through ego and express the spirit of irimi. But even when we learn how to make irimi in practice, we still haven't reached the highest mentality. We still need to be able to apply it in real combat. To reach that level, to understand the deepest sense or spirit of irimi, we have to overcome our human mental blocks. Because of that, I consider irimi to be the essence of Budo.

Kihon for Irimi:

We have a basic practice which is not actually irimi, but which teaches the hip movements that are incorporated into a realistic irimi practice. In a continuously moving, four-part sequence, begin with the right leg forward, left leg back.

1. Shuffle forward, moving your hip toward the opponent.
2. Turn toward your left, pivoting on your right foot to face the opposite direction while sliding your left foot to the rear, ending with the right leg forward.
3. Again shuffle forward.
4. Turn to your right. Pivot on your right foot to face the opposite direction while sliding your left foot to the rear, ending with the right leg forward.

You return to the starting place each time and can make many of these to understand the proper hip movement. Also make the mirror image to practice irimi from both sides.

Nagewaza (Throwing Techniques)

When we practice throwing techniques, we have to understand a few points. One, we have to respect the specialized throwing of judo. They are much more skillful, and their training is much more realistic than karate people's throwing, so you have to be careful. Second, before you practice throwing, you have to learn how to be thrown. You have to learn ukemi. You have to know what you are going to do when someone throws you. Physically, you should not get damaged. Mentally, you shouldn't panic when somebody throws you on the ground.

When you throw your opponents, first you've got to make exact timing. Timing is a key. Second, you have to keep your body close to your opponent, so that only one piece of paper can fit between you. Third, your body and your opponent's body have to become one, so that you can use your opponent's power and momentum. You have to feel what your opponent is feeling by becoming one with your opponent. Think how your opponent is feeling as he is being thrown. That way you have to train.

It is important to practice nagewaza which, with irimi, are some of the most difficult and advanced movements in kumite. Try not to be mechanical in performing these techniques. These movements are the expression of a certain mentality. You must decide not to step out of the way when your opponent attacks you. You must move in to your opponent.

Throwing techniques are primarily for sandans practicing for the yodan test. However, throwing techniques are very effective and realistic, and every black belt should pick one throwing technique as a favorite and practice it.

[More of the throwing technique information is in the kihon section about nage no kata.]

Iai (Drawing)

Iai is closest ma, with the sense of trying to catch the opponent's starting. You are not in the ma, but at closest ma, meaning you cannot get in even a quarter of an inch more. If you do, you lose. You and your opponent get as close as you can, where you both still have a chance to get out from the opponent's attack.

Everybody should learn this kumite practice. The basic idea is quite simple. Practice to find the closest distance from which you can avoid a kick or a punch. Comfortable distance is too far. Both sides make natural stance at the closest distance. Attack chudan oizuki with Ten No Kata form or any other agreed on attack such as maegeri. Defend by turning the body to avoid the attack.

Iai is similar to the Western cowboys' duel, so American people already know iai very well. Of course, the ma is different because we don't have a gun, but the cowboys stood in natural stance with a strong standing leg. They tried to find the most effective distance, each watching for the opponent's decision, then trying to draw quicker than the opponent.

In our iai, you have to move with the hips. Fist and hips have to go into the opponent. Many people are throwing only the fist, but iai is not just a touching game. That is the weakest part of most people's iai.

If you touch your opponent with your fist by twisting your hips or reaching out and you don't have a dynamic hip movement or strong standing leg, it doesn't mean anything. You have to avoid trying to just touch the opponent's skin. That's the worst kind of attack and the enemy of iai practice. When you touch, you have to be able to destroy the opponent completely. You have to try to make that kind of attack.

Hips have to go into the opponent. And you have to eliminate any minor motions that might signal your decision to move. There are many preceding things which are very important. Feel your opponent and the right distance, consider timing and how to reach him. Create a realistic atmosphere and strive for an ideal distance. If all of these conditions are met, it should naturally eliminate any telegraphing movements.

In iai we have the term "ki, ken, tai" which means literally "feeling, sword, body." In karate we have no sword so our fist is our "ken" to make "feeling, fist, body." When we make iai, all three must move as one.

In iai we practice to steal our opponent's breath. When your opponent is at the weakest moment in his breathing, try to get in with your strongest breathing. That is the actual, realistic iai attack.

When you make the closest ma, and the opponent tries to take the advantage by making the first attack, you can catch the moment he decides, evade the attack and simultaneously destroy the opponent. That is the idea. The key is to read your opponent's mind.

Iai is a practice for one of the most dangerous situations. For example, in the past assassins usually tried to kill other people by getting very close to them. At closest ma, the opponent can come at any moment with a one-motion attack and you have to be ready. Inside the ma, there is no chance of avoiding a first attack made without any minor movements; you will lose.

Obviously, if you feel the opponent coming into the ma, you've got to destroy him then. However, the immature mind miscalculates and, if you start to attack before he comes in, you will also lose. You have to be strong and mature. You cannot miscalculate this ma. That's the reason for practicing iai.

Practice

There are some other aspects of practice that are not directly tied to katas, kihon or kumite, but they are very important for making a sincere practice in a good atmosphere. The most important point is that no matter where we are or what we are doing, when we practice, we try to express our best.

Our understanding of karate comes when we make many strong practices and special trainings. We need to practice until our techniques come out naturally in front of opponents without conscious thought. Then we know that we really understand them. Everyone is capable of reaching this strong mentality. One big step is to focus your mind on practice every minute that you are training. Eliminate all of your other thoughts and concentrate on just your practice. Look at your mind honestly and strictly all of the time.

Master Funakoshi said, "Do not think karate is only in the dojo." Every day we have the opportunity to face ourselves very strictly. And even though we are disappointed with ourselves most of the time, because we don't improve very quickly and always seems to come back to the original level, we still don't give up. Even when we face ourselves very strictly, sometimes we feel that we are weak and stupid and everything seems hopeless. Then we have to apply all of our training, naturally and strongly to go through this critical time. That's why we practice.

Rei, Lei (Salute)

Whenever you practice, we say you must start with rei and end with rei. Rei is the bow you make at the beginning and end of class, the bow you make to your seniors before and after you demonstrate a kata and the bow you make to your opponent at the beginning and end of a sparring match. Rei reflects the formalized mentality and manners we use in our practice to create a good atmosphere, a sincere mentality and warm feelings.

Practice has to be natural, effective and realistic, but in order to continue to train, we have to make parts of it formalized to help pass on some understandings. The feeling of rei is one of these.

Keep a sincere mentality and don't salute without feeling. A lack of feeling is a weakness in modern people and society, when formality is only for appearance and there is no sincere feeling inside. As martial artists we need to understand the true importance of rei. So, when you make rei, do it with a humble, warm feeling and the right manner. The correct form will come when you have the correct feeling.

Many Japanese write rei with an R, but rei is exactly the same character as lei, an old Chinese character, so rei and lei are the same character. In Japanese there is no "R" or "L" sound. They are the same sound, but it is closer to the old Chinese character of lei. So lei and rei are both ways to spell the same thing.

Healthy Practice

We always need to ask ourselves, whenever we are practicing, why are we doing this kind of practice and what are the original feelings of the human mind, the natural movements of the human body?

Many beginners come to ask me, for example, is this angle 90 degrees or 45 degrees, or why does my senior say to do it this way but the other senior says another way? If my answer contradicts something their instructor has told them, they get confused. But for all of us, even beginners, if we really search for basic understanding of the human mind and human body, most of the time we can answer these questions clearly.

Karate practice has to make us healthy and strong. We also know that karate practice has to be realistic and effective. We have to repeat techniques over and over before they become realistic. To make even natural techniques like stamping kick effective may take a few years. You have to kick every day over 200 times, 70,000 kicks a year. In three years you will have made about a quarter million kicks. That is the minimum to understand this technique. The problem comes when the kick we are practicing starts to hurt some part of our body before we even reach 100,000 times. We will never be able to understand the technique. There is something wrong with that training and we have to avoid that kind of practice.

We need some maturity when we practice. For instance, sometimes people stick with techniques which obviously damage their health because it is the fashion and everybody is doing it. It may look fancy or they may see it in the movies and want to copy it. But they are looking at it with an immature mind.

When an opponent comes to attack you, you have to express your own strength to protect yourself. If you injure yourself in your practice before you ever face an opponent, you are already the loser. Therefore, we do not allow any basic practice that can damage ourselves or others.

Sophisticated and Primitive

There are different sides to our practice. One side is a very traditional, sophisticated kata practice and the other side is very natural and primitive. I don't mean barbaric. I mean vigorous techniques that everyone can use like uraken and fumikomi. I think originally all apes used movements like these as powerful attacks.

Techniques in karate have been formalized in basics and in katas through many generations of practice. But some of our techniques have not been formalized and still have their primitive, natural form. These techniques are powerful, as they are based on original human strengths. We should not consider them unrefined and without value just because they are simple. We cannot get so sophisticated that we reject good, natural, simple things.

Uraken is one of the best of these techniques. The last few years, I have been asking brown belts at Sunday practice to make uraken, and I was quite shocked to see that most of them have a problem making a natural uraken to a target.

I thought that most human beings could do this kind of very basic technique without much training. All apes know how to make uraken and fumikomi, but I have found that modern human beings are so far from the natural physical movements of our ancestors' caveman era (maybe 50,000 years ago, I don't know exactly) that they can no longer execute these natural fighting techniques. Maybe everybody lost this sense very recently.

Today, in many places it is fashionable to practice only tournament techniques. Too many techniques are ignored either because they are not suited to a tournament situation or because they are hard to master. The true effectiveness of techniques becomes less important because the emphasis is only on scoring a point. A tournament is not the same as a real fight. In the original martial arts practice, where we practice for a real situation, the effectiveness of each technique is of paramount importance. This is a point we must consider carefully.

Many important parts of our basic training have been almost completely eliminated by the newer generation because of the tournament system. Uraken is one of the most ignored, yet one of the most realistic and effective techniques in orthodox karate practice and in actual combat.

I hope that all students will develop and polish uraken as one of their favorite techniques.

I think we need to keep a realistic viewpoint of techniques. We must preserve these treasures and ancient knowledge in our practice. Therefore, I'm now teaching two very different training methods in our practice. One is a sophisticated kata practice; the other is primitive, like a simple uraken practice.

Special Training

Special training in Japanese is gasshuku which means accommodate together. We eat together. We sleep together. We train together. In English we use the term special training to remind ourselves that this training is somehow different from what we do every day in the dojo.

Think of the practices we make. I'm sure most junior members who go to special training suffer when they make a strong kibadachi for one and a half hours. And I hope everyone faces themselves straight and honest. Then, when you go back to special training each time, try to find out how you can make an even better kibadachi. Everybody should make special trainings that way for many years.

Everybody remembers that we do 1,000 oizuki at night, but I know that many times we are so sleepy or tired that we just think about how soon the practice will be over. Thinking like that we can't make even one good oizuki. When we make this nighttime practice, each oizuki has to be our best. We have to discover some of our weak points, some good feeling and learn how to enjoy finding the best way to make it. One night, just visualize your ideal oizuki. I suggest you compare this thrusting motion with the similar motion of thrusting with a spear. Imagine you are holding a long spear and the opponent is an armed samurai and you are penetrating with the point of the spear. Then try to understand the simple movements of hips and the way to make the best stance and how to connect both underarms.

Sometimes people ask when they should go to special training. I recommend that people who have been practicing at least three months should try to go. Beginners should know all of the basic blocks, punches and kicks. They should also know the order of the five Heian katas, Ten No Kata and basic ippon and sanbon gumite. White belts and brown belts learn a lot at each special training and should try to make as many as they can. Your first special training is very important. Think of it as jumping into a dark pool of water at night and be ready for anything.

I hope that all Shotokan members will attend at least one special training because this is the essence of traditional martial arts practice. It is unfortunate when a member quits training before attending special training because he will never understand the real meaning of our practice simply through daily training in the dojo. Even if circumstances force a member to stop training, he will have grasped an important part of practice by completing a special training.

Before special training, in preparation for it, I hope that all members will watch their diets closely, being careful of what they eat and drink, and will ensure than they are in good physical condition. People who are overweight should attempt to trim down. Also, people who have never run should start running beforehand, but be careful of blisters. Do not go if you have an illness or are overly fatigued from some other activity. Mentally and physically, it is important to be in good condition. It is not necessary to worry, as everyone is capable of completing special training, and worry will only worsen your physical and mental condition.

Once special training is over, if you have to drive a long distance to get home, be very careful because you are more tired than you think. Also, don't go back to normal living conditions right away because you may have problems if you don't give your body time to recuperate. Keep your mental strength up but take it easy for a few days or at least one day.

Participants attending their first special training get a shock from special training, and maybe they don't want to think about training for a little while. That's natural. It's very difficult to go back to the dojo the next day. But some people with strong minds go back to the dojo and continue with the feeling they got at special training. We emphasize that mental attitude in our practice is the most important thing and, although special training is only three or four days, sometimes it's worth more than four months or one year of regular training. Don't expect results immediately, though. Real understanding comes much later. It may take a few months to see the effects.

Most of the karate trainers in Japan or Europe or America don't understand special training or why we are doing this. Maybe they are confused, or laugh at us, but only people who have the experience of continuing to go back to special training can understand what we are really doing. We are learning to face ourselves honestly and strongly.

We have examples of people who have made exceptionally strong special trainings in the past. When we look at their accomplishments, perhaps we can see how much more we can try.

Four hundred years ago two kendo masters of the Eishin-ryu school made a special training. These two made a practice in front of a god of martial arts at the Kashima Shrine. They drew their swords 113,870 times in a sitting form practice. About 1940 a modern sword master from the same school tried to see how many times he could draw and cut with his sword the way the old masters did it. He could make it 100 times an hour but could not do it faster than that. This modern master could do this seven days, maybe ten, but the masters of 400 years ago could do it for 50 days. A human being is capable of that much.

The second incredible record was made about 150 years ago by the kendo master Yamaoka Tesshu. He made a ten day standing special training. Usually, kendo students made a three day standing practice where one junior had to attack his seniors and make 1,000 points a day. (There were ten seniors taking turns facing the junior.) They started at six in the morning and continued until six in the evening. After three days most juniors started to pass out, but Tesshu continued for ten days.

Mentality at Special Training:

At special training we start by learning how to face ourselves straight and honest and strict. But the mentality itself starts to change, year by year. For instance, when we reach about twelve special trainings, we get into what I call the "stupid behavior period." These are my own personal ideas, and the exact number of special trainings is based on my own statistics.

What happens is some black belt starts acting crazy at special training, jumping around and yelling at juniors. Juniors look at him and say, "This guy is crazy." I look at him and say, "He's been to special training around ten or twelve times." Almost everybody starts to behave in a very stupid way at this time. They're not stupid, but their behavior is funny. You know why? When we start going to special training, when we realize that our seniors are really strict and straight and honest, then we really try our best. But every time we're so tired and start to have regrets and say to ourselves something like, "Next time I'll go to the beach." At around ten times we start to get out from this stage and, suddenly, there is not so much mental pressure. We say to ourselves, "Wow! Special training is really good, I feel great!" And we want to make a demonstration in front of juniors who have really big mental blocks about special training.

So when I lead special training, I call over all those people who have ten or fifteen special trainings and I ask them, please don't behave in a stupid way, because juniors will misunderstand you. I didn't say this in the Special Training Notes, but actually this is the really notable breaking point. We call it removing one mental block.

When we reach around fifteen or twenty special trainings, this terrible special training experience is not that important any more. We start worrying about other people. How are other people doing? Before we were busy worrying about ourselves, but after around twenty times we get to another level. I'm always really happy to see this.

On the other hand, sometimes people get used to the practices and finish many special trainings and say to themselves, "Oh, I did it twenty or thirty times." If they only learned how to cheat themselves and are not making their best practice from beginning to end, they are wasting their time. It's not the number of times that is important. It's the number of times that you make your best special training that counts.

I believe that, as seniors, we are trying to reach a level where we are always facing ourselves straight and strict and honest. I don't say that anybody actually reaches that level. Reaching there is a little too much for us to say. We are trying to reach there, this is the important understanding. We are trying to reach there every year, to come back to special training and try to make our best. Still we have to come back again and again and try to reach that level. That's why we respect as a senior somebody who tries his best for many years.

At special training we don't worry so much about our belt rankings. Real seniority at special training means *continuing to try* to face yourself; continuing to participate in special trainings. This participation itself has meaning and value. There is no automatic seniority based on the number of special trainings we attend. It is this mental attitude itself, this *process* of trying to reach a high level. We don't consider that we have reached that level, and we love and respect our seniors for *trying* to reach that level. This is not ranking or colored belts. It's the way we can keep growing.

I hope each time you make special training everyone keeps up a good spirit until the very last punch. At this moment you will see yourself wake up in your life. If you can live every second like special training, you can have moments when you can taste your life. So, when you suffer, you thank heaven that you can really feel this moment. Your mentality, the deep part of your mind, your willpower or subconscious comes up very clearly. You can see yourself straight, strict and honest. That is what special training is all about.

Mental Blocks

Many people, especially around brown belt level, feel that their practice is not improving even though they are working very hard. There is this wall that they cannot break through. Even though they hit this wall many times, still they can't seem to make any progress. These people are actually looking at themselves with very strict eyes. It is really that their ability to see themselves in practice has gotten better, not that their practice has gotten worse.

They are not satisfied with their practice and so they push themselves harder. With this attitude, improvement will come, even if the person cannot see it himself. If you feel like you are not getting better, the best thing is to not worry and just keep practicing. Listen to your seniors and maybe even ask for their advice to see if there are any specific problems that are holding you back.

Other people, actually just the opposite, think that they are making a really good practice and are already a very high level. They can't understand why other people can't see how good they are. This is an immature attitude and it means that their practice is not improving as much as they think. They still have a long way to go.

To get out from your mental blocks, your fears or lack of confidence, you have to look straight ahead. No matter what happens, you look straight at the opponent. That's the beginning of facing your mental blocks.

Mokuso (Meditation)

When we make mokuso or any other meditation, we try to bring out our inner strength by being free from our consciousness. However, it is difficult for us not to be conscious. So when we make mokuso, in the beginning we concentrate on our breathing. Breathing is the best channel we have to connect the unconscious to the conscious.

When you sit with the right form, your feeling has to be in the tanden (the area under the abdomen). When you inhale, the feeling goes to the tanden, exhale through the nose quietly and slowly, but with a strong feeling. Do not fall asleep. You cannot tense any part of the body. Relax.

Some day you will find that you're not thinking of your breathing at all. At that time you are completely out of your consciousness, yet you are feeling very strong and pure. We consider this the ideal mental state for expressing ourselves because the mind and the whole of existence become one.

Vital Points

Vital points are points on the body where a technique is especially effective. The difference in effectiveness between an exact vital point and a nearby point is so great that an attack on the vital point may be as much as one hundred times more effective. In a real situation it is important to maximize the effectiveness of our techniques and hitting exact vital points is one of the ways we can do that. Understanding vital points is especially important for a smaller, lighter person.

We study vital points by knowing exactly what part of the body we are attacking and always making our target a very small pinpoint. Then the attack can be very effective. If we miss the vital point, the technique may not be effective enough.

So, there are two parts to this practice. First we must know the exact vital points. Second we have to train so that each execution of our techniques is to a precise point. Even when we can hit the exact point hundreds of times in practice, in real situations it is still very difficult to hit the pinpoints. If you miss the vital points in your practice, you have almost no chance in a real fight. We have to train to hit precise points, and we have to know and study about the location of these vital points.

I hope all senior members, especially sandans and yodans, know how to execute techniques to vital points. Even shodans and nidans should begin to learn how to do this.

In the martial arts, we always start with the understanding that when a strong opponent comes to destroy us, we have to defend ourselves, we have to destroy our opponent. Learning about vital points is one of the practices to learn how to do that. However, martial arts do not stay at that level and we have to understand another level where we are going to reach out to help or rescue other people — where we have to learn to resuscitate people who are unconscious. It is not necessary to be a medical doctor, but as a human being we have to always be careful and humble to understand human life and how to keep healthy and strong and live a long life and especially how to help other people to do the same. That's not another field. This is the goal of the martial arts and learning about using vital points to heal is part if this practice.

Therefore, if you hurt, for instance, your finger, it is not enough to just massage your fingers or knuckles. You have to consider all the vital points so that you can learn how the injured part is connected with all the vital point lines. These are what you have to find out by yourself. We use our own legs or arms to learn how to cure our injuries and help ourselves and then we are ready to help other people. So when you study vital points, be sure you keep both goals in mind.

Making Yourself One

In the beginning when we practice, we emphasize the following points. At first we look at eyes, pulling hand and hips. Later we study breathing to connect the mind and the body and research ways that the mind can lead the body as we face opponents. This is what we work on to reach the point where mind, body and feeling all move together as one to make the best expression of our strength.

Eyes

When we practice, we emphasize many things such as strong stances and tight underarms. More important than any of these things we practice are our eyes.

Eyes or eye contact is not simply looking. Eye contact indicates your mentality. When your mentality is weak, you cannot correctly see your opponent and it is impossible to concentrate. Thus it is important not to blink unnecessarily or look down.

First you must look at yourself to see what habits you have. There is a saying, "The eyes are the windows of the mind." You can look at your own mentality by being aware of your habits with your eyes. The actions of your eyes show your mentality.

Always in the martial arts, we emphasize our own mental state. Mental state comes to the eyes. The eyes always reflect or show directly how we feel inside. Therefore, keep your eyes open, level and never look down, never blink, never turn your head and show your immature, weak feeling, especially in front of opponents. Look at your opponent's eyes, but don't stop there. Use your strong mentality to look into his eyes and see his mind.

If there is no opponent, as in basics or katas, keep your eyes at your own eye level. Don't look down at your toes or look to the side to see what other people are doing. Don't criticize your movements or stance with your own eyes when you are trying to practice techniques. Keep your eyes connected to the opponent's eye level. This is the first important point in making yourself one.

Pulling Hand

You have to pull the pulling hand exactly to the point above the hip bone on the side of the body. In the beginning it is very difficult to be conscious of the other side of your body when executing blocking or punching techniques. For example, if you make oizuki or block with the right hand, you forget the left hand. When you use the left hand, you forget the right side. Therefore, always emphasize the pulling hand to connect both sides of your body. The pulling hand contributes unconsciously to developing the strength of the underarm. The underarm is connected to all basic techniques.

Hips

We have to be conscious of our hips which are the laziest, slowest and heaviest parts of our body. We emphasize the stance, back stance and front stance and then shifting hips back to front, front to back. You have to continue practicing moving your hips and try to reach the level where your hips follow your strongest feeling.

If you want to know about your hips strength, think about what happens when you shut your car door from outside and it doesn't close completely. You turn around and bump it with your hips. You don't push it with your hands or arms because you know it is very difficult to close the door and your hands and arms are not strong enough. Instead, you use your hips.

The center of human strength is the hips. All other movements have to go with the motion of the hips. Someone who moves his hips idealistically we call a strong man, an expert.

There are two reasons why we traditionally emphasize low hips in Shotokan. First, all strength comes from the hips and low hips are stronger than high hips. Second, is a realistic situation, when you become psychologically scared, the stance has a tendency to be higher than in a practice situation. It is important to maintain a low hip level in practice so that in real time the hips will remain relatively low. The person who can keep his hips low shows his mental strength. Therefore, it is important to keep the hips lower than the opponent, especially if contact is made.

Originally the mainstream karate practice in Japan emphasized rotating hips as the most important practice. A rotating hips movement is a very dynamic, very powerful motion when done simultaneously with the final form. This means your mind, body movement and stance all work together with a strong, dynamic hip movement. Sometimes try practicing with a makiwara or bag to examine how differently udeuke, tetsui, mawashigeri and uraken connect with rotating hip movements.

Back Foot

The back foot is a very important element for expressing our maximum strength in all of our techniques, especially thrusting techniques such as front punch and reverse punch. At the moment the technique touches the opponent, the foot must be solidly connected to the floor with the back heel down. If the foot is not in a strong position, the power of the technique escapes from the back foot.

Elbow

The elbow must stay inside the body's line to express your strongest techniques especially when we execute blocks such as udeuke (forearm block), tetsui (hammer block), and shuto-uke (sword hand block). When the elbow goes outside your body's line, there is no way to make these blocks work against a bigger, stronger opponent. You just can't connect all of the parts of your body together.

Connecting All the Parts

This is one way to train strong arms, underarms, hips and legs. First, we hook each other's wrist facing each at about 45 degrees in kibadachi and then execute attacks and blocks. If you use power in your shoulders or try to do this with your elbows out, within a few minutes you'll be really tired. That means you're using power in the wrong way. If you use your underarms, with your elbows in and make hip movements with the right stance, even after a long time you can continue to do it.

This not only makes your punch more powerful, but you also learn how to make techniques with a connected elbow and both underarms which are, in turn, supported by your strong kibadachi stance.

Breathing

Breathing is the connection between our subconscious mind and our conscious mind.

There is a saying:

A weak man breathes at the shoulders.

An ordinary man breathes at his abdomen.

A courageous man breathes at the tanden (lower abdomen).

A true man breathes at the feet.

We can see this for ourselves. When you are sad, you let out a big sigh and almost forget to inhale. When you are scared, you breathe up at your shoulders. You inhale and forget to exhale. We learn how to breathe through experience in practice, without words.

Mind Leads the Body

I want to talk about the first moves in Heian Shodan to explain what I mean when I say that in our ideal techniques the concentrated mind leads the body.

When you are standing at the start of the kata, imagine your opponent coming from the left side to kick you. When you make the first down block, imagine destroying the opponent's leg or ankle. Each time you attack with oizuki, feel your fist penetrate the opponent's solar plexus, like an arrow or spear. If you strongly imagine that, your mind is leading your body and you naturally breathe and move the ideal way.

With the attack, exhale as if you were shooting a jet of high-pressure air right at your opponent through a tiny hole in your fist. That kind of breathing penetrates the opponent and your strong feeling moves your hips forward. If you feel very strong and very courageous, your hips will start to move naturally. Imagine your opponents and concentrate to bring your strongest feeling first, then perform the kata.

Remember that the body does not move first with the feeling following and it is not enough to just use your conscious mind to think about the move. The breathing is the way to reach the subconscious mind and join it with the conscious mind to make what we call concentrated mind. Concentrated mind where conscious mind and subconscious mind get together as one mind is central to our practice. In the beginning we don't know what it is or how it feels but practicing this move in Heian Shodan is one way to start to find the concentrated mind.

Favorite Techniques

You will never be able to face anyone with confidence in a real situation if you don't have a favorite technique that you know will always work for you. You will always be uncertain of your chances.

You should feel comfortable and you should have confidence in your favorite technique. Take the time to practice it a lot so that it is part of your subconscious and is always available. Do not always depend on scheduled practice. Make your own training schedule for your favorite technique.

Many junior members ask whether it is better to practice every technique during one training session or to concentrate on one or two specific techniques. When practicing in the dojo with your seniors, do all techniques, as they teach you. (In 1981, when I wrote this suggestion, many seniors would lead all the basics at every practice. At best, the students would make a little progress in each one. Now in 1997, as I recommend, most seniors concentrate on one basic or a few basics at each practice, but they do many more of each one.) But even now when you are practicing by yourself, you should emphasize one or two techniques you can use against a bigger, stronger opponent. Always imagine a realistic situation. To really make a favorite technique effective you must practice it 200 times a day until you really understand it.

Seniors, especially, should practice your favorite movements or techniques until they are realistic and effective and you are confident to use them. This confidence makes your techniques work in a real situation.

One favorite technique is good enough, but if you have confidence in one, you can work on two or even three favorite techniques. Make each of them many thousand times, until you feel you can depend on each technique, and feel comfortable that you can do something no matter what kind of opponent you are facing.

Ma (Distance, Timing, and More)

Originally, all animals, including man, had a sense of ma. It is apparent that man would not have survived without this sense, but he has lost it through lack of experience in exercising the sense. We can redevelop a sense of ma, but not through discussion and intellectualization. We must experience it and be conscious of it to get it back.

There are five stages that we go through to discover ma. In the first stage ma just means distance. We look and say that we are two feet away from our opponent. When we practice basic sparring like sanbon and ippon gumite, we discover that ma is more than just distance. It also includes timing. That is the second stage.

In the third stage we start to notice that there is some other element besides distance and timing that I call alpha. What we notice is that the ma depends on who our opponent is. Between a particular pair of opponents the ma is usually very consistent.

The fourth stage is when we begin to understand the elements that go into the alpha. They include the nature of each person, their character, favorite technique, size and strength, background and experiences in life. All of these add together to make up the alpha that is part of ma.

In fifth stage, as we see expressed in the old Kendo thoughts, ma means rhythm, tempo and rank.

Distance in Martial Arts

One way to understand the differences between the martial arts is to look at the distance between opponents in a fight. The closest distance is in wrestling or sumo where the opponents grab each others' bodies. The next closest where opponents grab each other's clothing is judo. At the distance where the wrists or forearms touch is aikido. A little farther is where we don't touch each other to start a technique. That's our specialty in karate where we kick or punch. If it's farther than that, there is a weapon involved, small swords and swords, spears, archery, guns and cannons, all the way to rockets with atomic bombs.

With our specialty we attack opponents just before we close to the distance where we can touch. We have to feel what the opponent is going to do while we are outside that distance and be ready to move just as we reach our best distance (ma) for an attack.

However, I think it is not enough to understand our specialty. We also have to understand something about the other martial arts to make our practice complete. Throwing techniques almost disappeared in karate after it was exposed to judo. In Japan today, there are almost no throwing techniques in karate practice, especially for the younger generation. However, one may use throwing techniques as much as punching and kicking in combat. Because karate is a martial art, I put the grabbing and throwing techniques back into our practice with torite and nagewaza. Don't underestimate your opponent, though. If he is a judo-ka or a wrestler, we have to respect his specialty. If you give him the advantage of fighting at his distance, a judo-ka or wrestler can beat you very easily.

We make other changes when we face opponents with weapons. I think the jumping in techniques really started when karate went to Tokyo from the Okinawan Islands and kendo men joined the practice. This was especially true in the dojo where there is a flat, wooden floor, and it's much easier to jump in from a far distance. Before the kendo influence, karate did not use jumping-in techniques.

Sen, Sen-no-Sen, Go-no-Sen (Timing)

Sen, sen-no-sen and go-no-sen refer to the timing of attacks and counterattacks. In an engagement any of these timings may occur. It is important to study the different timings to understand when to apply each. In Japanese "sen" means first attack, "no" means of, "go" means late.

Sen means first attack. The first attack has a great advantage because when the opponent is not ready, you attack and destroy him.

Sen-no-sen means first attack of first attack. The opponent decides to attack, but you catch the moment of his decision and destroy him. Your mind is ready, just waiting to catch the opponent's decision to start and at that moment you attack. The opponent decides to destroy you, but in that moment you are already destroying him, that's sen-no-sen.

Your mind has to be like the surface of a lake in the mountains without any wind. If a cloud passes, the lake is already reflecting this moment, simultaneously. This very refined mentality is the same as the feeling for sen-no-sen. The opponent decides and simultaneously you go in. This is the essence, one of the first gates, of the finest understanding of the martial arts.

Go-no-sen occurs when the opponent comes to attack and you attack after the opponent's attack is finished. The best is when you are prepared to just evade or step back and make a vacuum between you and the opponent when the opponent comes to attack. Then you take the opponent.

You have to be awake when facing an opponent and the timing depends on the relationship between you and your opponent. You should be able to make all of these timings, depending on your relationship with your opponent.

Speed and Rhythm

Quickness exists because slowness exists. No one element can exist by itself. If you give your opponent a slow movement, you can then catch him with a quick one by changing your rhythm.

I think modern people execute the techniques much quicker than people practicing in the Okinawan Islands one hundred years ago. I was not there 100 years ago, but I can see, just in the last fifty years, people are changing the speed of the katas. For example, some schools, like Master Egami's, make Heian Shodan within 15 or 16 seconds. This is one type of practice.

Other times, Master Egami would teach moving hands from the left to the right taking 30 minutes with very slow movements. They were trying to understand what kind of mind we can prepare, what kind of mental stage we can be with very quick physical movements and with very slow physical movements.

After we begin to practice seriously, always imagining a real situation, gaining experience with kumite, we realize that speed is not objective, but subjective. In other words, speed is the result of a particular atmosphere between you and your opponent. People's mentalities, emotions, physical size, weight, past experiences and personalities are all elements that play a part in the perception of speed in physical movements.

Each opponent and observer of a kumite match will have a very different impression about the speed of the movements. Your actual speed is of secondary importance to your opponent's impression of your movements and speed. Ancient martial artists observed that speed does not exist by itself. In other words, quick movements appear fast in relation to slow movements.

Each one of us has to experience the difference between slow and quick motions, then we can understand what kinds of things are happening in our minds and in our bodies. When we are in a hurry, we feel like our minds and bodies are both moving very quickly, but that is not really true. When our body moves quickly, our mind moves slowly; when our body moves slowly, our mind moves quickly. It's like a spinning top, turning very quickly but almost standing still.

Master Funakoshi wrote in his book slow and quick, expand and contract, power and no power and, of course, we have these three elements, but there is something more we have to find. There is mental speed, mental rhythm.

In a real situation, how do you pull your opponent to your rhythm? By what? By your mental strength, your mental level. Therefore when you practice katas, always face yourself, and find your own best rhythm, your own best speed. When you make it quick, be quick; when you have to make it slowly, you take your time.

Some young people want to make every movement quickly and make the katas in such a hurry that they make a mistake. There are two things you don't have to do quickly: don't make your life short and don't make a mistake so fast. A mistake is okay, but the feeling of haste is one of the weakest expressions.

Grading

We make kyu tests in April and November each year. April 26th was the day Master Funakoshi passed away and November 10th was the day he was born. We make kyu tests during these months to remember those events. This is how I originally scheduled kyu tests, twice a year, in Southern California.

There are two points to always remember in a grading. First, we start with rei and end with rei. Second, the exam is not our goal; it is only one kind of practice for us. No matter where, no matter what, we have to express our best. This is the reason we continue to practice, especially people who get excited or who choke up in difficult situations like grading. They get in front of their seniors and cannot express their best. We practice so we can calm down. We want to be very alert mentally. Physically we try to be relaxed, with no conscious power in the shoulders and with our feeling going down to the lower abdomen.

When you present yourself to your seniors for grading, I am sure you feel excited or scared, but this is one of the important practices in karate. We have to get the habit of expressing ourselves strongly and making our best practice. If you don't have this habit, you need this practice to become strong and pass through these mental blocks.

As instructors, we have to remember we are human beings who make mistakes. We try our best not to make any big mistakes and always try to understand that, even though we are incomplete, we still have to do our best to reflect the level of our juniors. We have to realize that, as seniors, we are not perfect. We have a right to criticize juniors only because they ask us to.

Although we try as much as possible to be objective, our opinions are sometimes subjective, especially when a friend is taking the test. Automatically we see that our friend is very good. This wonderful friendship sometimes makes us blind to our friend's real level. No matter what intellectual level we reach, we can still be caught by this blind spot. We call this an immature mentality. Do your best to avoid this problem and look honestly at everyone with the same eyes. In dan tests, where there are other seniors, I advise you not to rank your own juniors at all.

Instructors should pay attention to their members' mental preparation, mental attitude, mentality itself. How can you find out? By watching eye movements and physical movements. These points are first in karate practice.

Then, humbly give the ranks to the juniors, knowing that you are not perfect. Of course, this doesn't mean that the junior can criticize the senior's decisions, because the junior is asking for the senior's opinion.

As always, I emphasize that the examiners must criticize their own teaching. If any juniors close their eyes or look down while they are making techniques or do not have the proper form, it is the instruction that has to be criticized.

Kyu Test:

In the kyu test we emphasize three points for kihon: eyes, pulling hand (hikite) and stance.

First, examiners are watching to see if you close your eyes or look down or turn your head. This shows an incorrect feeling and you should not do it. In kyu test, as always in the martial arts, we emphasize our own mental state. Mental state comes to the eyes. The eyes are the windows to the mind and always reflect directly how we feel inside. Therefore, keep your eyes open and level, facing your opponent and looking straight into your opponents eyes. Never look down, never blink, never turn your head and show your immature, weak feeling, especially in front of opponents.

When the opponent is in front of you, you cannot close your eyes or look down. But many people, when the opponent starts to come, close their eyes. When I first started to practice karate, if somebody closed their eyes or looked down, they got a punch right away from their senior. Today, I don't encourage any senior to do this, but all instructors must correct these bad habits in their juniors. When someone is looking down or closing their eyes, it shows they have a problem. Their mind is not strong enough. So I emphasize, always look straight forward and never look down.

Second, examiners are looking at how you coordinate right and left and left and right. A strong pulling hand connects underarms with other parts of the body to help make us one. We have to be one to make effective blocks, punches and kicks.

In the beginning it is very difficult to be conscious of the other side of your body when executing blocking or punching techniques. So make your pulling hand clear on each side (exactly on the point above the hip bone on the side of the body), make a fist, keep your shoulders down, slightly tighten your underarm and connect with the punch or blocks. This way you can execute techniques with good habits, using both sides of the body at the same time.

Third, they watch your standing form, mainly your back foot. Toes should not point outside and the heel never goes up when you execute basics. Also, don't think that front stance is standing with most of the weight on the front leg. Even in front stance we stand with the back leg; the front leg is light. The back leg must never be weak, there is strong contact with the ground and, yet, movement is free. You have to make a solid stance.

I ask the instructors to always make the basics in the order shown below so that we have a standard order and there is no confusion when members go to other dojos.

In every kata, along with the points for basics, you should show in the ready form before yoi, that your mind and body are ready to face the opponent. Each technique in the kata should be realistic and effective against your imaginary opponents.

In sparring you show your strong mentality by always watching your opponent's eyes. Make exact oizuki attacks each time and, when you defend, make clear, effective counterattacks. That's the correct feeling during kumite.

For examiners who have not given many kyu tests, you should be aware that, generally, beginners overestimate their own level. So you must explain, especially to beginners first experiencing a kyu test: be happy with 8th kyu. There is nothing wrong with 8th kyu and, if somebody who is very good is promoted to 7th kyu, then he is very happy. But if a beginner thinks he's a brown belt and he gets only 7th kyu, he's very sad and disappointed and soon disappears. We have to remember when we were beginners. We thought we were pretty good, but we didn't know how bad we actually were.

When I gave kyu tests at Caltech, I always told them that before my first grading I made four special trainings — two seven-day and two ten-day special trainings — and I received 6th kyu. If anybody practices harder than that and gets lower than 6th kyu, then they can come to complain to me. Actually, sometimes I felt upset with the results when I was coming up. The main practice for you when you take a test is not to feel bad even if you don't receive a higher kyu. We must be humble and trust our seniors when we take an examination.

The program for a kyu test is

Basic	Gedan Barai, Ageuke, Udeuke, Tetsui Uke, Shuto-uke Oizuki, Gyakuzuki Maegeri, Mawashigeri, Yokogeri Keage, Yokogeri Kekomi, Mikazukigeri, Fumikomi
Kata	A favorite Heian kata Another Heian kata as a request form. (One kata is enough for people grading for the first time.)
Kumite	Sanbon Gumite, Basic Ippon Gumite

Shodan Test:

The eyes show if the unconscious mind is moving or holding strong, so we emphasize eyes first and we never promote somebody who closes their eyes, turns their head or looks down. Also look at the other suggestions for practice in the kyu test.

I don't recommend Tekki Shodan as a favorite form for junior members taking the shodan test. I encourage junior members to practice Tekki Shodan but for the shodan test you should always select one of the Heian katas for your favorite.

You also have to practice lots of Bassai. All brown belts have to practice Bassai before passing shodan. We are asking brown belts to do it 5,000 times.

The program for a shodan test is

Basic	Gedan Barai, Ageuke, Udeuke, Tetsui Uke, Shuto-uke Oizuki, Gyakuzuki Maegeri, Mawashigeri, Yokogeri Keage, Yokogeri Kekomi, Mikazukigeri, Fumikomi or Maegeri-Fumikomi

Kata   Heian, one of these for a favorite form
            Bassai, request form

Kumite   Sanbon Gumite, Basic Ippon Gumite

Important points: eyes, stabilization of hips, rear leg, pulling hand

Nidan Test:

I hope all Shodans know continuous feeling when facing the opponent. These is no pause between block and attack. When you face the opponent, already your strongest feeling penetrates the opponent. Once you start to fight, you never stop until your opponent is on the ground. That's the spirit.

Execute block-attacks with one feeling, one breathing. Your mind must penetrate the opponent continuously. Don't disconnect your feeling or breathing in front of the opponent, in the opponent's ma.

It is important not only to have good, neat, solid form, but always to execute continuous techniques realistically and effectively. If your mind does not go strongly and continuously, your body will never be able to follow it. I'm not interested in some acrobatic movements of the body. Real martial arts training is very different from other types of physical performance.

All shodans have to practice Kwanku before passing nidan at least 5000 times, so all black belts are comfortable making Bassai and Kwanku.

A nidan candidate has to be a realistic, strong fighter. In addition to mastering the basic techniques, you have to have the ability to be a strong fighter in real combat, So kumite is jiyu ippon gumite and jiyu kumite. Emphasize distance, timing and focus.

The program for a nidan test is

Basic   Continuous Techniques: Gedan Barai Gyakuzuki, Ageuke Gyakuzuki, Udeuke Gyakuzuki, Tetsui Uke Gyakuzuki, Shuto-uke Jodan Nukite Chudan Nukite, Oizuki Jodan and Chudan, Oizuki Maegeri, Maegeri Maete, Maegeri Mawashigeri, Maegeri Yokogeri Kekomi, Maegeri Fumikomi Mawashigeri

Kata   Heian, Bassai, Tekki, one of these for a favorite form
            Kwanku, request form

Kumite   Jiyu Ippon Gumite, Jiyu Kumite

Import points: fighting spirit, realistic fighting abilities with a strategy

Sandan Test:

The torite in sitting and standing form is one of the Sandan candidate's projects. Movements from sitting form are the best training for dynamic movement of the hips. The Sandan candidate already knows basics and realistic combat, so these are extra exercises for certain situations encountered in real combat, such as when facing a judo or aikido man, wrestlers, boxers, or any opponent coming with certain unexpected techniques, distance or timing. So, in a way, the Sandan candidate has to be mature, to use his effective techniques against many different opponents.

Sandan candidates have to reach 5,000 times with Jion.

The program for a sandan test is

Basic   Leadership for beginners.

Kata   From 15 katas, favorite form
            Jion, request form

Kumite   Jiyu Kumite

Torite   Idori (sitting), Tachi Dori (standing)

Important Points: Sense of ma, strong feeling with calmness, no conscious power in shoulders.

Yodan Test:

Sandans practicing for the yodan test need to practice throwing techniques.

The program for the yodan test is

Nage no kata   Throwing forms (byobudaoshi, komanage, kubiwa, katawaguruma, tsubamegaeshi, yaridama, taniotoshi, udewa, sakatsuchi)

Applications   Throwing techniques

Irimi   Get into the opponent's body

Kata   Request form and favorite form

Kumite   Long Distance Jiyu Kumite

Important Points: Oneness of mind, fist and body (ki, ken, tai). Natural physical movements done humbly without concern for self.

Godan Test:

I ask godan candidates to train in iai.
The program for a godan test is

Kata   Free form (favorite form)

Iai   First movement of Ten no Kata from shortest ma as an attack. Evade or block opponent's attack.

Breathing   Tanden breathing

Kwattpo   Vital points, resuscitations

Important Points: Character

Fasting

This is a letter written to Reverend Mohri, the Chief Reverend of the Nishi-Hongwanji Temple in Los Angeles. It was written in January 1980, the seventh day of the author's annual week-long fast.

I am writing this letter to you about fasting and a menu to follow immediately after fasting as I promised to do last month. This is the seventh day of my fast, which I break tomorrow morning. I have lost 20 pounds in the process, and feel great mentally, but physically like an old man.

Twenty-eight years ago, when I started to make fasts, I was motivated by arthritis, which caused a cessation of feeling in my right leg. I found out that fasting made me feel better, and my stomach and abdomen, which were previously weak, became stronger. Also, my mind felt much clearer after fasting. I am now fasting as an annual event, and if I don't fast once a year, I feel that everything seems to go wrong.

A friend of mine in Japan, who was crazy about yoga, did a 31-day fast, but I was a young man who distrusted spiritualism and didn't feel that I had to go to a high mountain top or a special dojo to fast. I fasted in my own room, and at first I was disturbed by the many smells of cooking in my house. Before beginning my first fast, I read four or five books on fasting, and I chose some common elements from each in order to avoid making any grave mistakes during my fast.

1. Sick people, old people, small children and growing people, those with a temperature, flu, infection or skin disease should not fast.

2. On the day preceding the fast, eat only good, digestible foods in small amounts. Some people use laxatives to clear the abdomen. Food you eat will stay in your intestine all through the period of fasting, so there should be no bad-quality food in the abdomen.

3. During the fast, excessive movement should be avoided. Any twisting movement of the abdomen can be very dangerous. If you are careful when you stand up, sit down or lie down, there should be no problem.

4. One must drink large quantities of good quality, natural (not distilled) water, at least one liter per day. If you find that after three to four days you can't drink any more water because it is stuck in your throat, one drop of honey in your water should solve the problem. However, you must be careful not to mix anything else with water. Juice is not equal to water during a fast. If the mind weakens, the body must follow and nothing can stop it. If for example, the mind finds an excuse for drinking juice, it will rapidly weaken and the fast will be destroyed. If you introduce strong juices into an empty stomach, it can lead to bad results. The reason for this is that during a fast, all the fat and oil which usually accumulates on the inner lining of the stomach and protects it are removed by the fasting and acid may damage this lining.

5. All movements must be done slowly. If you perform any sudden movements, you may feel faint, your legs may weaken and you might fall.

6. For breaking the fast, great willpower is essential. If you eat large quantities immediately upon breaking your fast, you will destroy your physical condition and you will become mentally, psychologically and spiritually sick.

Included in this letter is my own personal menu for breaking a fast. Important points to remember are

1. You must eat good foods.
2. You must eat digestible foods.
3. You must eat small amounts of food and gradually increase the quantity.

If you fast for five days, you should take five days to go back to normal foods and normal amounts.

During a fast, you might have headaches, dizziness, nausea, palpitations, skin rashes or cold hands and feet. These are common occurrences. If you develop a skin rash, this means that poisons are being released from the body, then the fast can be considered successful. But if the abdomen is suddenly painful and you break out in a cold sweat, you must consider a twisted abdomen. Call a physician immediately, and you must go to a hospital immediately for an operation. This seldom occurs, but it is a possibility. This is the exception of exceptions, but you must avoid dehydration and a twisted abdomen. If you are sure to drink at least one liter of water per day, and are careful of your movements, this will not happen.

I don't want to lecture you, Reverend Mohri, but this is what I do during a fast — I sit [meditate], read and lie down. This practice of fasting will have a tremendous effect on your stomach and abdomen.

Sincerely, my best regards to your family,
Tsutomu Ohshima

Menu for Breaking Fast

1st Day

Breakfast: One cup of very thin vegetable soup with a very small amount of salt. This soup is composed of potato, carrots and onions, ground up and well cooked.

Lunch: One cup of thin rice soup with a small amount of dry bonito powder.

Dinner: One cup of soft rice soup with scraped dry bonito and two to three pieces of nori [seaweed].

2nd Day

Breakfast: Natural yogurt, one piece of toast without butter and one cup of soup.

Lunch: Oatmeal with milk and honey and a little bit thicker soup.

Dinner: Rice soup with 1½ cups of tofu with dry bonito and fresh applesauce.

3rd Day

Breakfast: Two pieces of toast, one soft-boiled egg, small glass of milk or orange juice

Lunch: A small amount of plain noodles.

Dinner: Rice soup, two pieces of nori, tofu and a small amount of broiled fish.

4th Day

Breakfast: Oatmeal with milk and honey, two pieces of toast, one soft-boiled egg, tea with honey.

Lunch: One bowl of noodles with one egg, one banana

Dinner: Soft rice, 1½ cup miso soup with tofu, small amount of fish with soy sauce and cooked vegetables.

5th Day

Breakfast: Two pieces of toast, one soft-boiled egg, one banana and tea with honey.

Lunch: Tuna sandwich, vegetable soup, juice.

Dinner: Ordinary food, but one half of normal volume, with no meat or fried food.

6th Day

Breakfast: One large glass of various fruit juices, mixed together in blender, two pieces of toast and tea.

Lunch: Ordinary food, one-half of normal volume without meat or oil.

Dinner: 70 percent of ordinary meal.

7th Day

Breakfast: Very easily digested, ordinary breakfast, slightly less than normal amounts.

Lunch: Ordinary foods, no meat or oils.

Dinner: Ordinary foods, slightly less than normal amounts, but no oil, meats or hard to digest foods.

After this, resume a normal diet.

Karate and Zen

Samurai culture has a strong Zen influence which is not completely religious, having been influenced by the martial arts. Both started Bushido, with its code that a man has to be absolutely right before he can draw his sword — as it cuts his own ugliness and stupidity — so that if it is used in the wrong way, the man cuts himself. The sword is justice and the basis of Bushido.

In both the martial arts and Zen, it is my understanding that what we are striving for is to eliminate any division or barrier between ourselves and the universe.

In martial arts we try to be as one, which is how we can express our maximum strength. This is very easy to say, but hard to do. Still, in our practice this is our goal. We try to be as one, both consciously and subconsciously, and also physically, mentally and spiritually.

I believe that Zen allows us to say that there is no ego, and that there is not only a universe outside ourselves but also a universe inside, and that all this is really one. This feeling, this stage, is the essence of Zen, and of the martial arts. There should be no distinction between the individual and the universe. The universe is in the mind and the mind is in the universe.

In modern times, the martial arts allow us to look at things simply as they are and provide a way for the mind and body to come together in practice. It is a basic and simple method and not a complicated Oriental mystery. You already have the crystal inside of you and are capable of passing through all of the levels and going quite far.

Dojo (Place of Practice)

We form a dojo to practice and learn together. In the dojo we pass on information. We push our juniors, our contemporaries and ourselves harder than we ever could if we practiced by ourselves. Each dojo has its own unique spirit and each member must work to make this spirit clean, strong and beautiful. The dojo lets us share a common experience from practice. We come to understand each other. With common experiences, we start to communicate with each other.

Think about katas. When we practice a kata as a group, we don't make the kata some way all our own. We try to make harmony with the group, encouraging other people with our best effort as other people encourage us. That's how we continue to practice many years and make many katas and many practices together.

The dojo is not a place where you try to destroy your opponents or show off your strength. This is one of the worst things, this very selfish, immature desire to show off to other people how tough we are. We have to be strict with ourselves to avoid this emotion whenever it comes up. Otherwise we hurt other people and other people hurt us. Then we cannot continue to practice. If we lose the proper spirit of practicing together, we damage each other before we can reach a good level. Instead, we need to practice with our friends in the dojo to make each other better. That is what our practice is all about.

Outside the Dojo

Please don't go out into the streets and get into trouble. Don't get into street fights. A real martial artist never fights with people of a lower mental level. Even in a bad situation we don't have to get upset and go crazy and damage other people. The best martial artist is never in a street fight in his whole life.

These days there are many crazy people and criminals and lots of violence in the streets. I hope my members will always be cautious about it. Don't get into a fight with these people. Your life is very precious and you cannot exchange it with such people. These people are not worthy to be your opponents.

Basically we're prohibited from using our karate techniques against ordinary people in the street. You never have the right to hit somebody first. Even if you think you have a reason, you don't have to get into a fight. As much as possible avoid such things in the street and, of course, with your family or friends.

Still we have to go back to the reality of modern society. We always have to be aware of where we are and who is around us. Never put yourself into a dead end kind of situation where it's impossible to face your opponent. We never start trouble and we try to avoid it from our side, but we always have to be prepared in case some crazy person or criminal comes to attack us. We have to be ready to escape or protect ourselves in any kind of situation. That's why we are practicing.

I tell my pitbull, Hippo, whenever I take him out, "You're a pitbull, therefore, even if you win, it is nothing. It is normal for a pitbull to win. So don't fight, ignore all stupid, little dogs who try to make trouble with you." Amazingly, he seems to understand me and he has never fought with any other dogs who are barking or coming to attack him. I believe all karate people should follow his example.

Karate-Do

This was written in August, 1981 for the twenty-fifth anniversary of the start of Nisei Week in Los Angeles.

Having taught karate here since my arrival as a foreign student in 1955, I have come to believe that American society truly possesses an amazing energy and great generosity.

I have wondered why the people of a nation which emerged victorious in World War II showed interest in the culture of the defeated nation of Japan, especially in karate which is an element of ancient Budo. While seeking an answer to this question, I have been given the opportunity to continue to practice karate, and through it I have been able to affirm my own attitude towards life.

What is Budo? Bujutsu seeks out methods to defeat an opponent on the battlefield. Budo, however, begins with the concept of "one's cutting of oneself" (onore a kiru). In other words, in Budo we realize that one's true opponent is oneself, and in constantly trying to imagine ourselves in the face of death, we seek to forge, harden and discipline our minds and bodies. In this manner we try to push on to the utmost limits of our strength. This is not the final goal of practice, though. What we seek through such training is to unshackle ourselves from external pressure and oppression and be truly free in will and action. Philosophically speaking,

Budo strives to make the leap from the relative to the absolute; and thus rising above the violence of the battlefield, it points the way to peace and harmony.

In other Oriental training methods whose goal is to heighten mental awareness, there is a dependence on books or on consciously moving the body or consciously controlling breathing. Budo, however, stresses the importance of actual experience and the training of the unconscious mind. For this reason, as much as possible, Budo avoids intellectual knowledge gained through words or sentences. Instead it stresses the union of mind, body and breathing while facing a opponent, especially in life-or-death situations.

To always face one's opponent directly means to face death directly. Budo demands the energy, spirit and strength necessary to criticize oneself strictly and honestly. Thus, through facing death every day, we can come to understand the difficulties we face in our daily lives; and through the daily practice of karate, we become able to cast away anger and fear. In this way, we can come to appreciate the value of an even, temperate mind (heijo shin).

The practice of Budo knows no boundaries of East and West, and recognizes no differences as to race or nationality. Someday in the near future, the essential concepts of Budo will become a part of the vocabulary of all languages. For example, those who are training in America have no problem in understanding the significance of "removing power from the shoulders" (kata no chikara o nuku), "lowering the hips" (koshi o otosu), "getting the right breathing" (kokyu o taitoku suru) or "the sense of ma" (ma no kankaku).

The practice of Budo will have great significance in the building of a new society in which, unlike the twentieth century where a man is evaluated by his wealth, new standards will be the strength, purity, warmth and richness of the mind.

Furthermore, the human relationships of master and disciple, and of senior and junior, so important to Budo, will come to play a significant role in future society. Such relationships must be based on the realization that only one's example can help others push themselves. Then the senior can lead his juniors with a warm heart, and the junior can respect his senior and follow him. In such a relationship, each must consider that he has three lives: his senior's life, his own and that of his junior. I see such relationships forming the vertical threads that will interweave as a fabric with the horizontal, democratic structure of western society. The emerging material, representing the qualitative changes of advancement in the evolution of the human spirit, will contribute to the creation of a new tapestry for future generations. Do means a "way" or "precept" that can be positively proved through experience. Budo's fate and true nature lies in the recognition and absolute affirmation of one's gains through experience. In striving to face one's opponent and one's death without deviation, there is no room for false or empty philosophy.

This is the basis for my belief that Budo has the quality to ensure it a place in world vocabulary. Relying on this belief and harboring no feeling of doubt, I have continued to practice for the past twenty-five years with the young people of the world.

Why We Practice

These were the opening remarks the author gave to the 1990 Shotokan Karate of America Convention.

I'm very happy to see all of you in 1990. We've been waiting for this year for a long time and now here we are. As you know, the world is changing dramatically, especially Russia and the Communist countries in Eastern Europe. America will change a lot in the next five to ten years, I can feel it. We are on the edge, between the 20th and 21st centuries, and we will need your mature mental attitude and your leadership to give what is valuable to the next generation.

We have some value as a group that we contribute to human society. We are not practicing volleyball or ping-pong or something like that. That is not enough for us. And if there is no value and we make only confusion, without improving our lives, only complaining and fighting with each other, there is nothing to pass on. If we are so self-centered that we only think of ourselves and our gain, today and tomorrow, then there's no reason for us to even get together. But we know something after going through many special trainings. We have some kind of unique feeling that can only be experienced through our practice and can't be exchanged with anything else.

I always talk about this with the senior leaders and I hope some of you some time will ask yourselves, "What are we practicing for?" That's been my desire from the beginning, that we make the reasons for our practice clear. Then when we get together, we can work on the things that are important, so that the next generation is happy to have this good atmosphere, this good mentality and can really appreciate their lives. That's the reason we have to work hard and train, to find the ways to carry on our practice. This is our reason for being together as a group.

Today, I want to emphasize three elements. First, we have to make life simpler. Don't forget this, especially dojo leaders and administrators. We should be getting rid of the junk in our lives, not creating more and more. And when we build the dojo in Carpinteria, if you sit there, even after a hundred or a thousand years, you still will be able to feel the simple design, the beautiful atmosphere. Then you will feel great, you will feel rich, even though you don't have anything. We have to find that one direction, towards a simpler life with no pollution, either mental or physical, and make the earth a clean, happy place to live.

Second, as we always emphasize, we have to face ourselves, straight and strict. That means that senior members sacrifice more than juniors. It is only because of the weakness of the human mind that people in positions of power in the world today become tough guys and take advantage of other people. Every white belt at their first special training makes one hour and a half in kibadachi. And although they try to avoid hardship or try to escape, still they have to face themselves. All of you with many special trainings know how hard it is to face yourself straight and honest and strict. Therefore, from beginning to end, I hope you are more strict with yourself than with any of your juniors, and never take advantage of your position for your own selfish purpose and never feel comfortable taking credit for somebody else's good will and efforts. That's how a senior should be.

Third, we have to understand clearly that we have to educate the younger generation, *on their level*, step by step. What I mean is, in human life, human history, we have gone from feudalistic systems to more democratic systems. In America and in other countries throughout the world, each of us has the right to say or do what we want to do, even if that means making a rotten thing. Of course, I don't include criminals or dope addicts, they are minus elements in society. But in martial arts, as in all human arts and culture, there are different levels, and only the higher level can feel the lower level. White belts cannot change the Dan Test because they don't understand it. But higher level people must not consider themselves privileged to be able to do anything they want either. Instead, they should think about the future and make a program to train junior members.

We always have to adjust to the junior's level, and make the target for them just a little bit higher than they can reach. Then they can come up, one by one. Our practice is not a place where we show off our own level, but where we communicate with our juniors and help them come up, step by step. You have to understand this educational system.

Finally, this organization is based on an academic purpose. Our practice is the most important element. According to the law, we have an administrative structure within the organization and we are required to have this meeting once a year. However, the academic direction comes first. This is not insulting the position of Jim Sagawa [President] or Don DePree [Vice President], but they know that no matter what happens in this administrative meeting, it cannot change our academic activity. It is the Black Belt Council that directs this activity, and each black belt in Shotokan Karate of America has a right to speak up. We have to make a line and give direction so that seniors and juniors can continue practicing seriously. That's what we're here to discuss.

So our organization is a little different from big corporations or government. We have to be careful to always simplify our administrative activities. We have to remember what is most important for us as a group and try to maintain this understanding all the way. If we do this, our society will have less problems, that's my opinion.

Our Goal for the Twenty-First Century

This was written in August, 1990 as a lecture for the Harmony 1990 gathering of Shotokan Karate practitioners from around the world.

We have to realize the historical fact that for 3,999,900 years of the last 4 million years, people have had to be strong to survive. Fighting behavior was natural for all living things, and was the most important instinct for survival. Human beings have won their fight.

Now we have to realize that there is no place for this violence because we do not need it to survive. We can no longer justify this behavior in society. But in our nature, in our conscious mind, if we stop this energy, man will become ill and abnormal. To keep peace, we must maintain this original fighting instinct.

In this reality, if we cut the fighting instinct, we are in an unnatural state. To create the next generation, we need this energy to be healthy. Otherwise the species cannot be maintained. If we use the fighting energy in the dojo, we can make people normal, strong and healthy.

In the martial arts the real opponent is not outside our own body. We must reach a high level, create real peace and maintain mutual respect. We must see each other like a mirror. Reach for the ideal mental state and make harmony with others.

Nobody can reach the high level at the beginning. There are stages in the progress of martial arts training. We have to train the next generation at their level of mentality. When they are young, people need the stimulation of competition. This is an important stage in maturity. But after the tournament stage, we have to be educated into the traditional martial arts training of polishing our characters and minds with physical training. We must know from the beginning of training what our goal is. We must find the value of our own existence, the value of our own lives and that this value was created by ourselves.

This is our place in society. This is where martial arts will be in the twenty-first century.

Afterword

Each year goes by so fast, but no matter how quickly time passes, we must continue to train harder, to polish and face ourselves, keep a strong and strict mentality toward ourselves and realize how lucky we are to be able to practice so many times. If you faced yourself strong and strict each time, you are blessed, but, if you didn't, don't wait. Start today, facing yourself strictly and honestly.

To polish means to face yourself straight, to recognize your weaknesses, to eliminate them and courageously step forward. This action, experience and practice is the only way we can free ourselves of our mental blocks, so that some day we will really be able to express our strongest, most beautiful energy on the earth.

I am always saying the same thing, but I'm sure you feel it. It's a miracle to be a human being, just to be alive. And to meet people is another miracle. I'm grateful to spend my life practicing karate with all my seniors and juniors. Every day is a wonderful, beautiful day. I'm sure you sometimes feel like that. I hope that until we say good-bye on the Earth, to the Earth, to all the people, to our friends and families, we will make something clean and beautiful and strong together, always keeping strict with ourselves and considering other people, from the beginning to the end of our lives. All of our discussion is based on this mentality, nothing else.

From the closing ceremony at the Harmony 1990:

I know I'm a very lucky young, old man. Even though I never write poetry, I become very sentimental when people die ... and I was thinking a few nights ago about this

huge, huge universe,
countless stars, this beautiful planet
and millions and millions of people ...
the changing times,
the passing months and years
in our short lives ...
the meeting.

We meet each other and I'm very happy because I met you.

Glossary

Some Japanese characters change sound depending on the character that comes before. When they are written in English, they are customarily written with the letter that comes closest to the sound. For example "keri" (kick) becomes "geri" in maegeri (front kick). This glossary has both spellings but the entry for "geri" will refer you to "keri."

ageuke up block, rising block
aorigeri crescent kick
ashibarai sweeping techniques
back fist uraken
back stance kokutsu dachi
barai *see harai*
bari-bari multiple attacks
basics kihon
begin hajime
block uke
bo long stick
bojutsu long stick techniques
bow rei, lei
brush block nagashi-uke

cat stance nekoashi dachi
chudan middle level
close-legged stance heisoku dachi
crescent kick mikazukigeri
cross-body punch kagizuki
cutting the distance ma-o-kiru
dachi *see tachi*
dan rank for black belts
distance ma
dojo place of practice
double block morote-uke
down block gedan barai
elbow attack enpi

enpi elbow attack
escaping techniques torite
evading sabaki
falling ukemi
focus of energy kime
forearm block udeuke
form kata
free jiyu (as jiyu kumite)
front hand maete
front kick maegeri
front punch oizuki
front stance zenkutsu dachi
fudodachi immovable stance
fumikomi stamping kick
gasshuku special training, literally "accommodate together"
gedan barai down block
gedan lower level
geri *see keri*
go-no-sen counterattacking after the attack is finished
godan fifth degree
goshin-jutsu self defense
gumite *see kumite*
gyakuzuki reverse punch
hajime begin
half-facing stance hanmi
hammer block tetsui
hand te
hanmi half-facing stance
harai sweeping technique, such as down block
head attack zuzuki
heisoku dachi close-legged stance
hikite pulling hand

hiza geri knee attack
horse riding stance kibadachi
iai sparring from closest distance in natural stance
immovable stance fudodachi
ippon 1. one-time, 2. full point
irimi getting into the opponent
jab maete
jinchu vital point just below the nose
jiyu free (as free sparing)
jodan upper level
jumping in tobikomi
jutsu techniques
kagizuki cross-body punch
kakiwake opening technique against a two-handed grab
kamae preparation or position
kamaete move into position
kara (as in karate) empty
karate empty hand
kata form
kata-te-dori escaping techniques from one-hand grabs
keiko practice (literally "to think of the ancient")
kendo training with swords
keri kick
ki mental energy
kiai expulsion of breath which focuses power, usually with a noise
kibadachi horse riding stance
kick keri (geri in some combinations)
kihon basic techniques
kime focus of energy

knee attack hiza geri
kokutsu dachi back stance
kumite sparring
kwattpo vital points, resuscitations
kyu ranks before black belt
kyusho vital points
lei *see rei*
long stick bo
lower level gedan
ma distance (and other elements)
maegeri front kick
maete jab (literally, front hand)
makiwara striking post
ma-o-kiru cutting the distance
mawashigeri round kick
meditation mokuso
middle level chudan
mikazukigeri crescent kick
mizu-nagare water flowing position
mokuso meditation
morote-uke double block
mountain posture yamagamae
multiple attacks bari-bari, renzuki
nagashi-uke brush block
nage-no-kata forms of throwing
nagewaza throwing techniques
natural stance shizentai
nekoashi dachi cat stance
newaza wrestling on a mat
nidan second degree
nukite spear hand attack
oizuki front punch
practice keiko
pulling hand hikite

punch tsuki (zuki in some combinations)
rank after black belt dan
rank before black belt kyu
ready position yoi stance
rei bow, salute to an opponent
renzuki multiple attacks
reverse punch gyakuzuki
rising block ageuke
round kick mawashigeri
sabaki evading
sanbon three time
sandan third degree
self defense goshin-jutsu
sen first attack
sen-no-sen first attack of first attack
shizentai natural stance
shodan first degree
shuto sword hand
shuto-uke sword hand block
side thrust kick yokogeri kekomi
side up kick yokogeri keage
sitting punch suwari-zuki
sliding in yoriashi
sparring kumite (gumite in some combinations)
spear hand attack nukite
stance tachi (dachi in some combinations)
stamping kick fumikomi
sumo style of wrestling
suwari-zuki sitting attack
sweeping techniques ashibarai
sword hand shuto
tachi stance

tanden the point in the body two inches below the naval, in the center from front to back

te hand

techniques jutsu

teisho heal of palm

tetsui hammer block (literally, hand hammer)

three time sanbon

throwing forms nage-no-kata

throwing techniques nagewaza

tobikomi jumping in

torite escaping techniques

tsuki punch

tsukuri fix, set up

uchikomi hammer

udeuke forearm block

uke block

ukemi falling techniques

up block ageuke

upper level jodan

uraken back fist

vital points kyusho

water flowing position mizu-nagare

wrestling on a mat newaza

yamagamae mountain posture

yame stop

yodan fourth degree

yoi ready

yokogeri keage side up kick

yokogeri kekomi side thrust kick

yoriashi sliding in

zenkutsu dachi front stance

zuki *see tsuki*

zuzuki head attack

Index

escaping techniques, 19. *see also torite*
evading. *see sabaki*
eyes, 8, 14, 59, 157, **212**, 224
falling techniques. *see ukemi*
fasting, **230–33**
favorite technique, 154, 171, **217**
fist, **93**
forearm block. *see udeuke*
forms. *see kata*
free one time sparring. *see jiyu ippon gumite*
free sparring. *see jiyu kumite*
front kick. *see maegeri*
front punch. *see oizuki*
front stance. *see zenkutsu dachi*
fudodachi, 16, 56, **73**
fumikomi, 20, 127, **129–30**
Funakoshi, Gichin, 5, 6, 11, 16, 29, 32, 34,
    35, 36, 39, 43, 52, 54, 56, 58, 68, 84,
    125, 146, 197, 222, 223
Funakoshi, Yoshitaka, 16, 56, 73
Gankaku, **51–53**
gasshuku. *see special training*
Gate of Heaven, 185, 192
gedan barai, 13, 19, 52, **78**, 92, 168
Goju, 75
go-no-sen, **220**
goshin-jutsu. *see self defense*
grading, **223–29**
    godan, **229**
    nidan, 35, **227**
    sandan, 55, **228**
    shodan, 31, 39, **226**
    yodan, 175, 194, **228**
gyakuzuki, 97, **98–100**, 110, 115, 117, 167
    and oizuki, 101–2
    application, 99
    from other stances, 100
    practice, 100
hammer block. *see tetsui*
Hangetsu, **43–44**
Hangetsu dachi, 43, **74**
hanmi, 77, 130, 164
harai-uke, 168
head attack, 133
healthy practice, 200
Heian Godan, **26–30**
Heian Kata, 11–30
Heian Nidan, 7, 22, 112
Heian Sandan, **19–21**, 111, 129, 190
Heian Shodan, 11, **13–15**, 191, 215

Heian Yodan, 7, **22–25**, 36, 87, 111, 136
heisoku dachi, 20
hikite, 15, 60, **213**, 225
Hippo, 236
hips, 14, 65, 76, 108, **213**
    low, 14
    opening, 149
    training, 109
hips movement, 31
hiza geri, **131**
horse stance. *see kibadachi*
iai, **195–96**
immovable stance. *see fudodachi*
injuries, 171
ippon gumite, 155
    with kicks, 121
irimi, 168, 192, 194
    kihon for, 193
Itosu, Anko, 11, 13, 39
jab. *see maete*
jamming kicks, 168
Jion, **54–55**
jiyu ippon gumite, 153, 171, **176–81**
    with ashibarai and nagewaza, 179
    with kicks, 181
    with maete, 181
    with tobikomi attacks, 180
    with uraken, 180
jiyu kumite, 153, 154, **171–75**, 177, 179
    close combat, 173
    control, 174
    long distance, 175
    slow jiyu kumite, 172
jodan, 154
jodan attacks, **169**
judo, 142, 144, 146, 173, 189, 190, 194,
    219
jumping in techniques. *see tobikomi*
Jutte, **45–47**
kakiwake, 24, **87–88**
kata, **5–58**
    incomplete parts, 7
    practice, 7, 35, 58
    start, 8
    starting, 14
kata-te-dori, 37, **190–91**
keiko, 1
kendo, 204
ki, ken, tai, 195, 229
kiai, 8